SUE TURTON

THIS
BOOK
WILL
(help you)
CHANGE
THE
WORLD

Illustrated by
ALiCE SKiNNER

wren
&rook

First published in Great Britain in 2017 by Wren & Rook
Text © Sue Turton, 2017
Design and illustration © Hodder and Stoughton Ltd, 2017
All rights reserved.
ISBN: 978 1 5263 6090 8
E-book ISBN: 978 1 5263 6091 5
10 9 8 7 6 5 4 3 2 1

Wren & Rook
An imprint of Hachette Children's Group
Part of Hodder & Stoughton
Carmelite House
50 Victoria Embankment
London EC4Y 0DZ
An Hachette UK Company
www.hachette.co.uk
www.hachettechildrens.co.uk

Printed and bound by
CPI Group (UK) Ltd, Croydon, CR0 4YY

Publishing Director: Debbie Foy
Commissioning Editor: Liza Miller
Art Director: Laura Hambleton

Designed by Mélanie Johnsson
Cover design by Anna Morrison

CONTENTS

PART TWO:
TOOLKIT FOR CHANGE....150

WORKING FROM WITHIN ALTERNATIVE FACTS ARE THEY TRUSTW
ON THE RISE IN THE WEST AT THE MOMENT? ARE THEY CREDIBLE?
ONQUER SOCIAL MEDIA SPEAK LOUD AND PROUD AVOID THE HYPNOTI
PLE OFF THE UNIONS? PROVIDE TEMPLATES FOR THE LETTER MA
TION AGENT SHARE YOUR CAMPAIGN ON SOCIAL MEDIA NOMINATIO
RM RELAX YOUR HANDS DO NOT FILL THE GAPS WORLD DEBATING CHA

VIST CASH FOR QUESTIONS WHO IS BEHIND THIS? INDIAN ELECTIC
WER IS THE SYSTEM BROKEN? PROVOCATION EXAGGERATION MONITORIN
NGING MINDS WORKING FROM WITHIN ALTERNATIVE FACTS ARE TH
HY IS POPULISM ON THE RISE IN THE WEST AT THE MOMENT? ARE THE
YOUR STORY CONQUER SOCIAL MEDIA SPEAK LOUD AND PROUD AVOID
NG YOUNG PEOPLE OFF THE UNIONS? PROVIDE TEMPLATES FOR TH
R VOICE? ELECTION AGENT SHARE YOUR CAMPAIGN ON SOCIAL MED
CROSS YOUR ARM RELAX YOUR HANDS DO NOT FILL THE GAPS WORLD
WHO IS BEHIND THIS? INDIAN ELECTIONS OF 2014 TO SLANT T
? PROVOCATION EXAGGERATION MONITORING FERGUSON DO THEY HAV
ROM WITHIN ALTERNATIVE FACTS ARE THEY TRUSTWORTHY? EDIT
IN THE WEST AT THE MOMENT? ARE THEY CREDIBLE? GET YOUR M
IAL MEDIA SPEAK LOUD AND PROUD AVOID THE HYPNOTISTS CRACK
E UNIONS? PROVIDE TEMPLATES FOR THE LETTER MAKE YOUR GO
T SHARE YOUR CAMPAIGN ON SOCIAL MEDIA NOMINATION FORM THE
YOUR HANDS DO NOT FILL THE GAPS WORLD DEBATING CHAMPION COMES

IVIST CASH FOR QUESTIONS WHO IS BEHIND THIS? INDIAN ELECTI
OWER IS THE SYSTEM BROKEN? PROVOCATION EXAGGERATION MONITORIN
ANGING MINDS WORKING FROM WITHIN ALTERNATIVE FACTS ARE T
WHY IS POPULISM ON THE RISE IN THE WEST AT THE MOMENT? ARE TH
YOUR STORY CONQUER SOCIAL MEDIA SPEAK LOUD AND PROUD AVOID
JING YOUNG PEOPLE OFF THE UNIONS? PROVIDE TEMPLATES FOR T
ER VOICE? ELECTION AGENT SHARE YOUR CAMPAIGN ON SOCIAL ME
R CROSS YOUR ARM RELAX YOUR HANDS DO NOT FILL THE GAPS WORL

QUESTIONS WHO IS BEHIND THIS? INDIAN ELECTIONS OF 2014 T
STEM BROKEN? PROVOCATION EXAGGERATION MONITORING FERGUSON DO
WORKING FROM WITHIN ALTERNATIVE FACTS ARE THEY TRUSTWO
ON THE RISE IN THE WEST AT THE MOMENT? ARE THEY CREDIBLE?
ONQUER SOCIAL MEDIA SPEAK LOUD AND PROUD AVOID THE HYPNOT
OPLE OFF THE UNIONS? PROVIDE TEMPLATES FOR THE LETTER MA
TION AGENT SHARE YOUR CAMPAIGN ON SOCIAL MEDIA NOMINATIO
RM RELAX YOUR HANDS DO NOT FILL THE GAPS WORLD DEBATING CHA
OLD ACTIVIST CASH FOR QUESTIONS WHO IS BEHIND THIS? INDIAN
ON SUPEPOWER IS THE SYSTEM BROKEN? PROVOCATION EXAGGERATION MO
GHT CHANGING MINDS WORKING FROM WITHIN ALTERNATIVE FACTS

INTRODUCTION

THE WORLD
IS FULL OF
PEOPLE
WHO DON'T

LET'S CALL
THEM 'THE
VOICELESS'

My name is Sue Turton, and I've been a TV reporter for more than 27 years, breaking exclusives and dodging gunfire. In 2014, I had to take on the might of the Egyptian regime when I was falsely convicted of terrorism charges along with a number of Al Jazeera colleagues, three of whom languished in prison. I started the #FreeAJStaff campaign, causing one hell of a stink in Cairo and helping to get my fellow journalists released. This is a book for people who are equally mad about something and want to get their voices heard.

The voiceless are passengers on the planet, happy to sit and watch the world go by as the bus of daily life trundles along. Even if they see something out the window that really bothers them, they're never going to push the stop button, jump out and speak up.

But there are others on our planet who do. They're the ones who shout out, who frantically hit that stop button and jump off the bus to make a difference. They have one hell of a voice!

Can your lone voice make much of a difference, we hear you ask? It really can. These are some young people who spoke up and helped change the world ...

STUDENTS FIGHT RACISM

In September 1957, nine black students enrolled in an all-white high school in the US state of Arkansas. They were challenging racial segregation in American public schools. Their stand signalled a key turning point in the fight for black equality.

14-YEAR-OLD ACTIVIST TAKES ON SUPEPOWER

Joshua Wong was 14 when he realised the Chinese government was forcing his Hong Kong school to teach a skewed version of history. His campaign to fight against the propaganda grew into a national movement – known as the Umbrella Revolution – bringing hundreds of thousands of Hong Kongers out on to the streets to protest.

GIRLS AGAINST ASSAULT AT GIGS

In September 2015, 17-year-old Hannah Camilleri and a group of her friends in Glasgow set up a social media campaign called Girls Against. It was to raise awareness of sexual harassment and assault at music gigs after Hannah revealed that she'd been attacked at a concert of the band Peace. Their campaign prompted many more victims to speak out and got bands, venues and security companies working together to make gigs safer places.

These young activists were once sitting right where you are now, wondering if their voice was enough to change the world. And look what happened.

According to polls, most of the young people who voted in the EU referendum wanted to remain: 75 per cent of 18–24-year-olds. A decision affecting the future of the country was swung by older generations because more of them spoke out, were taken seriously and went out to vote. And leaving the EU is just one example of many: young people's views are frequently dismissed or undervalued.

The good news is, the tide may be turning. The youth vote contributed to Theresa May's humiliation in the 2017 general election by mostly backing her main opponent, Jeremy Corbyn. The surge in young people registering to vote is making politicians everywhere sit up and listen.

Clearly, amazing things can happen when you put your mind to it and come up with a plan. That's where this book can help.

First,

knowledge is power. If you know how this world is currently being run, you can work out how to change it. We'll examine the system's strengths and also its weaknesses – those things crying out for change.

Then,

we will find the best methods to deliver your message: should you work within the system and get involved with politics, or channel your motivation into protest on the outside?

But having a plan is only half of it ...

you also need to be as effective as possible at every step. So we've got you a gift: a shiny, smart, fresh-out-of-the-box toolkit. It will help make sure that you have all the right facts, can gather allies from near and far and that your voice really makes a difference – giving you the tools to help you change the world!

PART ONE

In the first part of this book, we'll bring you up to speed with the way the political world works at the moment and identify how activists can make a change. You might decide that the current system needs to be turned on its head, but knowledge is power – if you know how the decision-makers operate, you can work out how and where to strike.

CHAPTER ONE :
KNOW THE SYSTEM

To take on the system, first you have to understand it. So, here are some basics.

The UK is a democracy. That's a type of political system and it's the envy of a lot of people all over the world – especially those who have no say in how their country is run. Democracy comes from two Greek words: *demos* meaning people and *kratos* meaning power. Smack them together and you get a political system that relies on free elections to choose the decision-makers. If you think about it, that's kind of awesome. Street-sweepers, science teachers and billionaire landowners all get one vote each. Everyone is equal when standing in the voting booth.

It's not until you think about what life is like for people who don't live in a democracy that you appreciate the freedoms democracy brings.

Take, for instance, freedom of expression — our right to speak openly and even to criticise the government. People started revolutions in the Arab Uprisings of 2011 because they were not allowed to speak out.

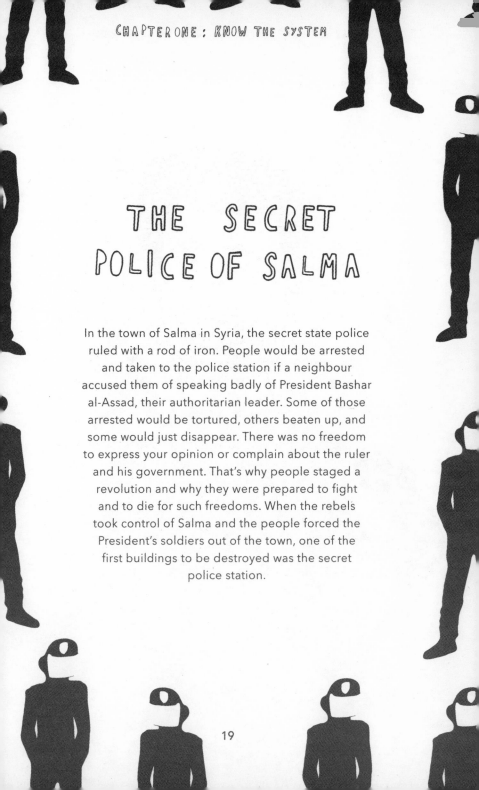

THE SECRET POLICE OF SALMA

In the town of Salma in Syria, the secret state police ruled with a rod of iron. People would be arrested and taken to the police station if a neighbour accused them of speaking badly of President Bashar al-Assad, their authoritarian leader. Some of those arrested would be tortured, others beaten up, and some would just disappear. There was no freedom to express your opinion or complain about the ruler and his government. That's why people staged a revolution and why they were prepared to fight and to die for such freedoms. When the rebels took control of Salma and the people forced the President's soldiers out of the town, one of the first buildings to be destroyed was the secret police station.

NOBODY SAYS THE DEMOCRATIC SYSTEM IS PERFECT BUT IT DOES TRY TO GIVE PEOPLE A SAY IN HOW THEIR COUNTRY IS RUN AND IT ALLOWS PEOPLE TO SPEAK OUT AGAINST THEIR RULERS.

So how does our democracy work?

In the UK, our democratic system is split three ways:

THE EXECUTIVE
THE LEGISLATURE
THE JUDICIARY

The Executive is another way of describing those in power, from the prime minister at the top all the way down to city mayors. They write laws and run the country.

The Legislature is made up of the two Houses of Parliament – the House of Commons (filled with MPs we elect) and the House of Lords (filled mostly with people that governments appoint). These two Houses go over each new law proposed by the government with a fine-tooth comb, and keep an eye on each other too.

The Judiciary is responsible for the court system that ensures everyone in our democracy sticks to the rules. They include the bigwigs, such as judges in the Supreme Court, the country's highest court, as well as the magistrates who volunteer for their local communities. Some democracies, like the USA, have a written constitution – a formal set of laws for the judges to follow. But the UK doesn't have one; instead, decisions are based on rulings from earlier legal cases, sometimes

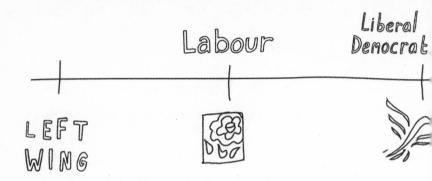

going far back in history. The reason this system of democracy is genius is that each of these powerhouses oversees the other. That means none of them can get carried away and wield too much power.

Who's in control of the government?

The government is usually controlled by one of two political parties. In the UK, the two main parties are the blue Conservatives and red Labour – adversaries that have been slogging it out for more than a century. Traditionally, people in the UK used to vote according to their social class. The working class voted Labour and the middle and upper classes voted Conservative.

The Labour Party grew out of the trade union movement and was founded in 1900 to rival the Conservative Party. It promoted workers' rights and benefits and introduced the National Health Service in the 1940s. The Labour Party is left-wing and believes that taxing the rich to help the poor by providing benefits is the fair thing to do. Labour is known for supporting government services

CONSERVATIVES

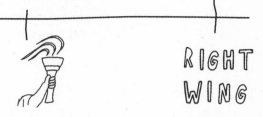

RIGHT WING

such as the NHS, a minimum wage and those struggling in society. Many in the middle and upper classes can face heavy taxation on their wages to pay for the government services championed by Labour. Those people have traditionally relied on the Conservatives to cut spending on the 'welfare state' – the system of government services that tries to protect the health and wellbeing of citizens.

The Conservatives, also known as the Tories, are right-wing and historically the party of capitalism and business. They're seen to be supported by captains of industry and the more comfortable sections of society. The Tories think that if somebody works hard and becomes rich, they deserve to keep their money – and their success story will inspire other people to work hard too. They think that businesses are more efficient and better judges of what society needs than an interfering government.

Sitting between Labour and the Tories are the Liberal Democrats – the yellows – standing for personal freedom and equality for all. They believe that by encouraging business a more open society is achieved. The Liberal Democrats are in the middle of the political spectrum. They're in favour of high taxation, but want to use it to pay for the NHS and other government services rather than giving benefits out to the poor.

Blurred lines

However, these positions on the political spectrum have got a bit blurred in the last 30 years or so. For example, far fewer workers head to factories, coalmines, shipyards and steelworks to earn their pay today. And people often don't think of themselves as working or middle class.

Margaret Thatcher was prime minister from 1979 to 1990. Her policy to allow council house tenants to buy their homes went some way to blur these lines. It made many working class families who were able to become homeowners think differently about their political stance, making them more supportive of Tory policies. Then another PM, Tony Blair, moved the Labour Party into the centre-ground with a much more capitalist-friendly approach. He reduced the amount of influence the trade unions had on Labour.

Today, it's much harder to guess which party someone might support based on their job or the size of their house. In fact, during the 2017 general election, there was lots of support for Labour among the middle classes while many in the working classes backed the Conservatives. And of course, there are many other political parties that candidates can stand for. These smaller parties are often very popular in certain areas of the country or with people who are passionate about a specific issue.

DEMOCRATIC UNIONIST PARTY

Currently the largest party in the Northern Ireland
Assembly. It wants Northern Ireland
to stay part of the UK.

GREEN PARTY

A left-wing party that particularly
promotes environmental issues.

PLAID CYMRU

A left-wing party that wants Wales
to be an independent country.

SCOTTISH NATIONAL PARTY

The biggest party in Scotland. It wants
Scotland to be an independent country.

SINN FÉIN

Currently the second-largest party in Northern
Ireland. It wants Northern Ireland to become
part of Ireland.

SOCIAL DEMOCRATIC AND LABOUR PARTY

Another party in Northern Ireland that wants
it to become part of Ireland.

UKIP (UK INDEPENDENCE PARTY)

A right-wing party founded on the desire
for Britain to leave the European Union.

ULSTER UNIONIST PARTY

A party in Northern Ireland which wants
Northern Ireland to stay in the UK.

Who are we actually voting for in a general election?

That would be the MPs, or members of parliament, in the House of Commons. The UK is divided into 650 areas called constituencies. There are roughly 70,500 people in each. These constituencies are often called seats – some are considered 'safe' seats because the majority of residents in those constituencies always vote for the same political party. Other seats are a bit less stable because voters there are more likely to change their mind, and often vote differently in each election.

Each seat elects a member of parliament who promises to speak up for the interests and concerns of his or her constituents. Every five years or so, the prime minister calls a general election. That means Parliament is dissolved (a bit like the end of a school term) 38 days before the election and the MPs' jobs are up for grabs. Most MPs will go back to their constituents and ask to be voted back in, but some may choose to step down. Candidates from other parties (or people standing by themselves, called 'independents') can now put themselves forward for the job too. The political parties and all the candidates use these 38 days to try to persuade the voters that they would be the best people to run the country – or, at least, to be in charge of their constituency. All parties write what is called an election manifesto (a long-winded essay that lays out how everyone's lives would be better if their party was in charge) explaining what they would change by bringing in new policies. The candidates then head out on the campaign trail. This means they walk around the streets of their constituencies, smiling and shaking hands, kissing babies, drinking warm pints and listening to voters' concerns.

Of course, their constituents might take absolutely no notice of what the local candidates say. Voters could decide whom to choose based on the national leaders of each party – perhaps based on their performance during a TV debate. They might pick a party based on their policies concerning local issues like schools or housing. Or they might just vote the way their parents voted.

How do people actually vote?

There are three ways you can vote, but the most popular method is to go to your local polling station. If you're over 18 and you've registered with your local council, you will get a voting card in the post about a week before the election with the address of the temporary polling station you should visit. The polling stations are open from 7 a.m. until 10 p.m. – you just collect a ballot paper and take it into a small booth where you can secretly mark a cross next to the candidate of your choice. Drop your ballot paper into a box at the front desk and you're all done – a member of our democracy using your voice. The other ways are to nominate someone else to vote on your behalf if you cannot attend the polling station on the day, or to vote by post.

Counting the votes

The winner of the election is the party whose candidates take more than half of the 650 seats in Parliament. However, in order to win a seat, a candidate does not need to receive 50 per cent of the votes cast in that constituency – they just need to win more votes than any other candidate. This system is known as first past the post. Sometimes no party wins more than 50 per cent of the seats, in which case we have a 'hung parliament'. That means the biggest parties have to try to convince the smaller ones to make a pact to form a government together. It also means there's lots of arguing about which policies each party is willing to compromise over – they need to agree on enough topics to form a government. This happened after the 2010 general election, when the Conservatives and the Liberal Democrats went into government together in a formal coalition.

The Tories called the 2017 general election expecting to increase their majority (because the polls predicted a Conservative landslide) – but the opposite happened. Theresa May's Conservative party ended up eight seats shy of an outright win and had to find new 'friends' to achieve a majority. She did a deal with the Democratic Unionist Party – a right-wing party in Northern Ireland – which added another ten seats to the Conservative total in exchange for a billion-pound cash injection. It isn't a formal coalition, but the DUP has promised to back the Conservatives in key votes.

How does a party then run the country?

The leader of the winning party becomes prime minister. If it's a new prime minister, they move into 10 Downing Street the day after the election. First, they visit Buckingham Palace to talk to the Queen. Her role is 'head of state' – putting her in the same rank as the president of the United States – but in the UK, it's mostly a symbolic role because the prime minister calls the shots. However, it's still up to the Queen to formally ask the new PM to form a government. The PM will go on to visit the monarch each week throughout their term in office, allowing her to express her views on government matters – though she very rarely intervenes. Regal formalities out of the way, it's then time for the PM to pick some of their own party's MPs to help them run the different government departments.

How do they decide who does what?

The prime minister is the boss. They're the head of the government and responsible for all policies. They're also in charge of the civil service – a small, politically neutral army of people which puts the government's policies into practice and does the day-to-day organisation.

The prime minister has around 21 top jobs to give out. These include heading up various government departments, known as ministries. As well as running a ministry, each 'Secretary of State' also gets to be a member of the Cabinet, the prime minister's inner circle and the most powerful decision-making body in the country.

These are the big Cabinet jobs:

**Chancellor
of the Exchequer**
Sorts out the budget
and decides what the
country can afford.

Home Affairs
In charge of policing,
immigration and
national security.

**Foreign and
Commonwealth Affairs**
Leads diplomacy
with other countries.

Defence
Plans how to
protect the UK from
overseas threats.

Lord Chancellor
Oversees the courts
and the prison system.

Education
Sets policies for schools
and universities.

**Exiting the
European Union**
Works out how
to leave the EU.

International Trade
Helps UK businesses
succeed overseas.

**Business, Energy and
Industrial Strategy**
Oversees UK industry,
our energy supply
and environmental
protection.

Health
Sets policies
for the NHS.

The Cabinet usually heads to Downing Street on a Thursday morning to discuss government policies and make decisions.

What about the opposition?

The opposition is the political party with the second highest number of winning candidates in the general election. The leader of the opposition is the leader of that party. It is the opposition's job to carefully watch how the government is behaving and hold them to account. It forms a Shadow Cabinet with jobs just like those of the Cabinet – each shadow minister keeps a close eye on their assigned department and challenges the Cabinet minister if they do something wrong.

What do the rest of the MPs do?

They make up the House of Commons, also known as the Lower House of Parliament. It's their job to consider new laws and scrutinise the government's policies. The MPs who aren't government or shadow ministers are called backbenchers. These backbenchers are sometimes new MPs gaining experience and keen to be promoted to ministers, and sometimes they're experienced MPs who enjoy being a thorn in the government's side, asking difficult questions and holding them to account. It might look like a very old-fashioned place with leather seats and lots of ornate woodwork, but strip away all that pomp and plushness and the House of Commons is really just a big room full of people trying to get their voices heard.

The Speaker

You can easily spot the Speaker in the House of Commons – they are constantly yelling 'Order! Order!'

The Speaker is in charge of the debating chamber – they get to choose who is allowed to speak. The role is held by an elected MP who then puts their name forward for the Speaker's election. If they are chosen by their fellow MPs, they have to become politically impartial so they do the job fairly. This means they have to resign from their own political party and never express a political opinion again – even after they've retired! To be allowed to speak during a debate in the Commons, an MP stands up in what is termed 'catching the Speaker's eye'. They can also do it the old-fashioned way and write a request in advance.

If someone misbehaves by using abusive language or being deliberately disobedient, the Speaker can just ask him or her to be quiet or they can suspend the MP. They can even send everybody home if the MPs are too unruly to control.

THE BEAST OF BOLSOVER

In September 2016, the Labour MP for Bolsover – nicknamed 'the Beast of Bolsover' – was ordered to leave the House of Commons chamber after calling the prime minister 'dodgy Dave'. Dennis Skinner MP might be getting older – he was 84 at the time – but he doesn't hold back. Mr Skinner was referring to David Cameron and the money he had used to pay off his mortgage. Mr Cameron had avoided the same question previously, so Dennis was hoping 'dodgy Dave' might answer now. It turns out you're not allowed to refer to the prime minister as 'dodgy' in the chamber, but Mr Skinner was feeling rebellious. When the Speaker asked him to withdraw the word, the Labour MP mischievously replied, 'Which word?'

The Speaker said, 'The word beginning in D and ending in Y that he inappropriately used.' But instead of withdrawing it, 'the Beast' said the word again. The Speaker asked Mr Skinner to leave the chamber for the rest of the day for his behaviour.

Passing laws

The Commons is like a big, fat law-making factory. The winning party takes its election manifesto and draws up proposals for new laws. Proposals can also come from public inquiries, lobbyists, campaign groups and other parties. These proposals (also known as bills) are discussed in the House of Commons with MPs from all parties debating their pros and cons.

Generally speaking, a bill will only pass if the governing party backs it, since they have the majority of votes. Bills go through three stages, known as readings, in the Commons. If approved by a majority at the end of this process, they're then sent to what MPs call 'the other place'. This is how they refer to the House of Lords, the second debating chamber. In the Lords, there are more readings and possible amendments to the bill, at which point it gets sent back to the Commons for final approval. Once it's got that, it's put in a red box and taken to Buckingham Palace for 'Royal Assent' by the Queen – a formality where the monarch officially turns a bill into law.

So the House of Lords rubber-stamps the Commons' bills?

Not quite – the House of Lords, also known as the Upper House, double-checks the laws voted in by the Commons to ensure they are fair and practical. There are about 800 members in the Lords: around 90 are hereditary peers (they get a seat because their dad or mum had one), two don't vote but oversee ceremonies, and the rest are chosen by prime ministers.

The idea is that members of the public who are experts (such as former heads of the Metropolitan Police, or those who have done lots of important charity work) should act as a check on elected officials. They don't have the power to stop laws, but they can delay them and suggest changes. The Lords meet first thing each day to question government ministers on their work. Then they might scrutinise proposed laws or debate important topics of the day.

PARLIAMENTARY PING-PONG

The result of the 2016 Brexit (short for British exit) referendum created an almighty squabble between the two houses. The House of Commons sent the bill to trigger the UK's European divorce to be ratified, or signed off by, the House of Lords.

The Lords tried to make changes to the legislation, known as Article 50, sending back amended versions to the Commons twice. Each time, the Commons refused to include the Lords' suggested changes and returned the original bill. It looked like this parliamentary ping-pong would keep going but, in the end, the Lords backed down and the government got its legislation through unchanged.

Inside Parliament

Inside the huge Gothic Palace of Westminster, there are more than 1,100 rooms, 100 staircases and almost 5 km of passageways. On the main floor are the debating chambers, the libraries and the lobbies. The Central Lobby, shaped like an octagon, forms a busy crossroads between the House of Lords to the south and the House of Commons to the north.

The two debating chambers are easily identified – the Commons has green benches and the Lords has red ones. There are two red lines on the floor of the Commons 2.5 m apart. This is apparently just over two sword-lengths and was meant to stop heated debates turning into duels. However, MPs have never been allowed to bring their swords into the chamber, so it's a curious measurement! The clanging of the Division Bell sounds on TV screens, throughout the palaces and in pubs and restaurants around Westminster. It's the sign for MPs to hurry to the chamber to vote at the end of a session. They don't actually have to sit through the debate, but they do have to turn up to vote. More often than not, they've been ordered whether to vote Yes or No by the leader of their party.

The whips

Should MPs miss a vote, they'll be in deep trouble with the party whips. These senior MPs are in charge of party discipline. Think of a shrewd headmistress armed with a clipboard, ticking off attendance with a big bag of punishments should you fail to turn up and vote as instructed. Once they've made it to the chamber, each MP then files through the corridors to the right (in favour of the bill) or left (against the bill) of the debating chamber. They don't have to write anything down – they've voted just by walking through what are known as the Aye and the No Lobbies.

Scottish MP Kirsty Blackman and her young children were once 'caught short' as the bell rang out. Kirsty had taken her kids, Rebecca and Harris, to Parliament because the Scottish schools had broken up for the summer but her own summer holiday hadn't yet started. Business eventually done, they were forced to scarper to the division lobby with Kirsty just making it in the nick of time. She waltzed through the corridor still clinging to both children – this was most unheard of!

Taking a question to the people

Sometimes decisions are taken out of MPs' hands and given directly to the electorate to decide. This is generally on matters of how the UK is governed and is called a referendum.

To date there have only been three countrywide referenda – including the one held in 2016 which led to the decision to leave the EU: Brexit.

IS IT TIME TO LEAVE THE EUROPEAN UNION?

In 2013, prime minister David Cameron promised that if he won the next general election he would hold a referendum on whether the UK should stay in the European Union. He didn't want to leave the EU, but some in his party did – they had been calling for a referendum for some time and he wanted to keep them in line by settling the matter, because he was confident the Remain side would win. So in 2016 the Conservative government did as promised, and a nationwide referendum was held. Cameron got the result he really didn't want: with the highest-ever turnout for a UK-wide referendum (72 per cent of the eligible population), 51.9 per cent of the voters chose to leave the European Union. The decision frightened the moneymen. The worldwide stock markets lost more than $2 trillion in one day – the worst single-day loss in history – and the pound fell to a 31-year low. It cost Cameron his job; he was accused of misjudging the mood of the nation and resigned straight after the result.

WE MADE
A
EUGE
MISTAKE

NEVER GONNA GIVE
NEVER GONNA LET
NEVER GONNA RUN
AND DESERT EU

BREXIT MEANS BREXIT

GOODBYE EU - HELLO WORLD!

UP, OWN ND

It's worth mentioning that a referendum in the UK is not legally binding. Parliament is sovereign, which means it's in charge — so referenda are just very big opinion polls on what the country thinks. The government doesn't have to bow to the result. But to ignore the will of the people in a direct vote like this does kind of go against everything democracy stands for.

It sounds like the entire country is run from London!

It was until 1999, when there was a political earthquake in the UK. Following activism all over the country, powers were transferred to national regions across the UK. Devolution led to assemblies in Cardiff and Belfast and the Scottish Parliament in Edinburgh. People in Scotland, Wales and Northern Ireland now have greater powers over local education, health, agriculture and housing. Westminster still holds on to what are called 'reserved powers' in areas like foreign affairs, defence and the economy.

In September 2014, a referendum was held in Scotland on whether it should be an independent country. The turnout was massive — almost 85 per cent of the electorate turned up, with the No vote winning with 55.3 per cent of the vote.

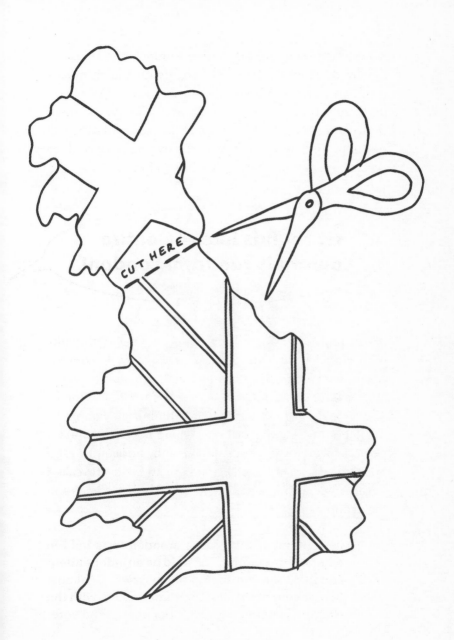

The system

So what do you think of the political system?

Now you know how it's set up and how it's supposed to represent you, does it do the job?

Do you know who your MP is?

If you don't, go to
theyworkforyou.com/mps
and enter your postcode.

Have you spotted things about the system
that are in need of an overhaul?

How would you change it
to make it better?

UNAPPROACHABLE
OUT OF TOUCH
ETONIAN OLD TRADITIONAL
IRRELEVANT OVERPAID
PARLIAMENTARIAN
LAMENTABLE DULL
ARROGANT

CHAPTER TWO: IS THE SYSTEM BROKEN?

The words on the left are just some of what's been said to describe politicians in the UK. They suggest a political system that no longer has the best interests of all its citizens at heart.

This chapter will dissect the UK's political landscape by examining spin doctors and lobbyists, voting systems and voting ages, ethics and corruption. It's time to lay bare some of the problems with our democracy.

Politics isn't relevant to young people

In 2013, then-MP Sadiq Khan said he didn't think young people's views were being taken seriously enough. He explained that if an MP was in a marginal constituency (one of those unsafe seats that are difficult to win) with a free hour to campaign before the election, they were more likely to visit a residential care home than a sixth-form college. And that's because MPs think old people vote and young people don't.

A 2014 opinion poll of 16–24-year-olds found that less than a third of young people were interested in politics. On the face of it, this seems like an odd finding. Young people have a lot to say about everything from tuition fees to climate change. It might be that the opinion poll asked a question that was too vague – perhaps young people care an awful lot about what goes on in the world, but they don't feel parliamentary politics can make a difference.

In the 1964 general election, over three-quarters of the population voted – and turnout was roughly equal across all generations who were eligible to vote. However, after that, youth turnout started to fall significantly. By the 2015 general election, only 43 per cent of 18–24-year-olds turned up to the ballot box.

But just two years later, a YOUTHQUAKE hit the UK – an election rumble that left the Conservative Party shaken to the core. With the opinion polls predicting a massive Tory majority, over a million young people quietly registered to vote. And on polling day, they turned out in force: more than half of all 18–24-year-olds voted, and 60 per cent of them voted for Labour's Jeremy Corbyn. While JC's scruffy image and his outspoken past bothered many older voters, he came across as genuine and down-to-earth to much of the younger electorate.

Since the Bite the Ballot group launched in 2010, more than five million teenagers have joined its campaign for greater political participation among young people. It has grown from a lunchtime school club into a national, youth-led movement that works within communities to encourage discussion. This debate can be online or in real life, and has led to young people conducting research that is often quoted by the media and politicians. When young people turn out and make their voices heard, decision-makers are forced to listen. And they're forced to take those voters into account when coming up with new policies. Politicians stay disengaged from young people at their peril!

Even though the youth vote turned out in style for the 2017 ballot, it was still dwarfed by the grey vote. 84 per cent of older people (those over 70) made their voices heard. So there is still loads of work to be done to encourage more young people to get involved.

This all leads to a few key questions:

⟶ Have you ever been taught about politics?

⟶ Has your MP ever visited your school
or workplace to explain what they do?

⟶ Have you ever been asked to take part in
a debate about political issues?

*At the moment, the answer is often No. But if it
became a Yes, young people would have a much
easier time getting excited about politics.*

Not all young people get a vote

If it was up to the Labour Party, the Liberal Democrats and the Green Party, then 16- and 17-year-olds could probably vote – these parties are all committed to lowering the voting age to 16. The House of Lords voted to drop it in 2015. And in Scotland, 16-year-olds could even vote in the 2014 referendum on Scottish independence. But the Conservative Party don't think that the 1.5 million 16- and 17-year-olds in the UK (2.2 per cent of the population) are politically savvy enough to vote. Actually, the real reason may be that the Tories think giving young people the vote would be a bit like turkeys voting for Christmas; political scholars have long held the view that we all start off with a left-wing, or liberal, attitude and get more conservative the older we become.

Back in the 1800s, British statesman Benjamin Disraeli was quoted as saying:

" *A man who is not a Liberal at 16 has no heart; a man who is not a Conservative at 60 has no head.* **"**

The scholars certainly seemed to get it right in 2017, when age proved to be the biggest indicator of voting intention. If it had been up to 18- and 19-year-olds, Jeremy Corbyn's Labour party would have won the vote by 47 percentage points! Meanwhile, among pensioners over 70, the Conservatives led by 50 points.

Taking younger opinions into account might well have changed the course of recent history. A 2016 opinion poll conducted on the day that the UK decided whether to leave the EU found that 82 per cent of 16- and 17-year-olds wanted to stay in Europe. At the other end of the age range, 58 per cent of over 65-year-olds voted to leave. If the younger people had been allowed to vote, the UK could well have stayed in Europe. Of course, that would only have happened if they had turned up at the polling station, but there is evidence that they would have done just that – by the coachload! The National Union of Students did a survey and found that 75 per cent of 16- and 17-year-olds said they would have voted given half a chance. After all, they'd have to live with the decision for much longer than those leave-voting pensioners.

Roza Salih is a young activist in Glasgow who helped set up a campaign for better treatment of asylum seekers when she was in school. She explains why she thinks young people deserve a voice at the ballot box.

II The voting age should definitely be lowered to 16. Why? Because if you are 16 and can join the army and fight for your country, why can't you have the opportunity to vote? In Scotland you can get married and have a family at the age of 16, so why not have a vote to elect someone who would be representing you and making decisions on your behalf? **II**

Politicians are out of touch and just want power

Who is the best person to represent your interests in parliament? Is it somebody who has experience of a working life before standing as an MP? Or is it someone who has worked in Westminster and knows how the political system functions? The latter sort of MP has often progressed from being an adviser, researcher, policy analyst or lobbyist. They are called career politicians and they're on the rise.

In 1979, just 21 elected MPs had only had jobs inside politics. By 2015, that figure had risen to 205. These politicians are often accused of being out of touch with voters. But the system does allow for MPs to talk to the people they represent every week. All constituents – the people an MP represents – can ask their MP for help at a weekly constituency surgery. It's a bit like going to the doctor, but rather than looking after your physical health and advising the best course of medication, the MP will listen to your problems and advise on a political remedy. Sometimes the requests stray from the expected or solvable to the bizarre:

MP for Welwyn Hatfield, Grant Shapps, was once called by a constituent and asked if he would load and **unload the removal van** at his new house.

Enfield Southgate MP David Burrowes was asked to **move a dead pigeon** seen on top of a bus shelter.

A constituent asked Vale of Glamorgan MP Alun Cairns to **feed his dog** while he was away.

A tearful constituent who had been dumped by her partner asked East Worthing and Shoreham MP Tim Loughton if he could **persuade the guy to take him back**

But does listening to constituents' problems mean MPs understand everyday problems? Many have been caught out with the question: 'How much does a pint of milk cost?' You won't be surprised to hear many haven't got a clue. So do MPs lose touch once they've been elected, or were they never in touch in the first place?

In 2010, 23 out of the 29 members of the new Cabinet were estimated to be millionaires. However, there are grounds for optimism. The 2017 general election result led to the most diverse bunch of MPs ever to walk into the House of Commons – there were rises in the numbers of female, LGBT and ethnic minority politicians. But let's not get carried away: women still only make up 32 per cent of MPs, and the proportion of MPs who went to private school is way higher than in the general population. There's still more work to do.

MPs get told how to vote – they don't make up their own minds

You would be forgiven for thinking 'political posturing' is a term to describe MPs who don't stand up straight, push their shoulders back and pull their stomachs in.

But political posturing is actually when an MP takes a political stand not because they believe in it but because it gives them or their party a political advantage. And this is often how debates are won or lost in parliament. The party leader decides which way the whole party will vote and then directs the party whips to make it happen. The whips send out a circular (a written instruction actually called The Whip) each week that tells politicians about upcoming parliamentary business. The debates are rated in order of importance. The very important ones are underlined three times – making it a three-line whip to attend – so the politician knows he or she needs to be there to vote. (Remember Kirsty Blackman dragging her kids out of the loo so she got to the vote in time?)

So MPs often don't make their own individual decisions about a bill – they're shepherded like a flock of fluffy white sheep through the voting corridor by the whips. It's called whipped voting and can sometimes stop an MP from acting on behalf of their own constituency.

Politicians can't be trusted

In 1994, a political scandal (see p.60) led to the then-prime minister, John Major, launching a big investigation. It ended in a 'standards in public life' review that set out seven principles for MPs to work by:

SELFLESSNESS   INTEGRITY

ACCOUNTABILITY   OBJECTIVITY

HONESTY OPENNESS

LEADERSHIP

Not that many people would use this list of principles to best describe today's MPs. In fact, trust in politicians, corporations and the media appears to be in freefall. According to the Edelman Trust Barometer (an opinion poll that measures trust and credibility), belief in Britain's core institutions is falling faster than Alice down a rabbit hole.

Both the election of President Trump and the plans for Brexit resulted in a plummeting of trust levels from the end of 2016 to the first week of 2017.

Many people no longer have faith that political leaders or businesspeople can fix the world's problems. Voters suspect that politicians are often not operating in the interests of their constituents. And they could be right – there's an awful lot of money swilling around, as you're about to discover.

Lobbyists have way too much power

There is one group of people whose profession is to persuade politicians to think a certain way. They are the lobbyists. Their name comes from the lobbies where the MPs hang out before and after debates and votes. Their job is to persuade MPs to vote in the best interests of whichever big company hired the lobbyists.

Lobbying is a multi-billion pound industry that can mean some MPs are approached by lobbyists 100 times per week. Companies pay a shedload to lobbyists to get their voices heard – Google spent over $16 million lobbying the US government in 2015. We don't know how much the tech giant spent lobbying the UK government, because under UK laws it doesn't have to publish that figure.

The lobbying profession got into deep trouble back in the 1990s when journalists started to smell something wasn't quite right in the way this lobby system was working. This was the political scandal that led to the Seven Principles of Public Life being set out.

CASH FOR QUESTIONS

In 1994, the owner of Harrods department store, Mohamed Al-Fayed, told journalists at the *Guardian* that a lobbyist called Ian Greer had been paying MPs to ask questions in parliament on his behalf. This was a blatant attempt to influence MPs and was against the rules. Al-Fayed said the MPs accepting these payments of £2,000 were Conservatives Neil Hamilton and Tim Smith. It came to light that Smith had taken undeclared payments of between £18,000 and £25,000 from the Harrods owner. Tim Smith decided not to stand in the next election, but Neil Hamilton was spectacularly defeated by independent candidate (and BBC journalist) Martin Bell, who stood specifically on an anti-sleaze ticket.

The shady world of lobbying still didn't improve much after that though. In fact, in 2010 the Conservative prime minister David Cameron promised a clean-up:

❚❚ *We all know how it works. The lunches, the hospitality, the quiet word in your ear, the ex-ministers and ex-advisers for hire, helping big business find the right way to get its way. In this party, we believe in competition, not cronyism.* **❚❚**

But his new 'clean' legislation only covered those lobbying a minister or permanent secretary (a senior civil servant). Politicians didn't have to admit to speaking to anyone else more junior in government. So how do politicians bypass these rules? If a lobbyist is asked by an oil company executive to get him a meeting with the energy minister, the lobbyist can call up a junior minister. That junior talks to the senior minister every day during the course of political business. So the lobbyist can get that junior minister to arrange a meeting with the oil company executive and nothing would be reported. No trace of lobbying – and no transparency.

The head of the Commons committee that scrutinised the new lobbying law spotted this loophole and said it was a 'useless dog's breakfast'.

Donating to a party gives the rich political influence

According to the Bureau of Investigative Journalism, in 2010, a £50,000 donation to the Conservatives would get you a face-to-face meeting with then-PM David Cameron. The investigators found that 60 donors gave more than £50,000 to the Tories.

But it's not just the Conservatives who are cashing in for access. In 1997, when Labour was in power, Bernie Ecclestone, then the boss of Formula 1, donated £1 million to the Labour Party and – surprise, surprise – soon afterwards, Formula 1 was made exempt from a ban on advertising tobacco.

None of the parties are likeable

Enthusiasm for the political parties has been sinking for decades. According to a 2015 NatCen British Social Attitudes survey, the number of people identifying 'very strongly' or 'fairly strongly' with a party dropped from 46 per cent in 1987 to 37 per cent in 2010.

The fact that people are fed up with parties means many are failing to turn out to vote. In 1950, voter turnout was 83.9 per cent of the eligible population, but by 2001 it had fallen to just 59.4 per cent. It did bounce back a bit in 2015 to 66.2 per cent, and despite warnings of voter fatigue after many elections in a short space of time, turnout rose even further in 2017 to 68.7 per cent. Still, the general trend seems to be that people are getting passionate about political issues, not political parties.

Elections are all about the leaders, not the policies

Election party broadcasts, televised leadership debates and election campaigns are devised to sway the voter into making their ballot decision based on party leaders rather than their local candidates. Desperate for votes, the leaders can become caricatures of themselves, with dress sense, holiday destinations and relationship histories all coming under the media spotlight. The policies they support often take a back seat.

Looking for proof? On the day before the 2015 general election, the Sun newspaper devoted its front page to the way Labour leader Ed Miliband ate a bacon sandwich.

In the run-up to the 2017 election, the Conservatives looked at Theresa May's high opinion polls and made her the party's main selling point; her election bus slogan was 'Theresa May: For Britain', with only a very small print mention of the Conservative Party. The Labour Party saw Jeremy Corbyn's low opinion poll standing and took his name off their battlebus.

But in a weird twist of fate, May's image deteriorated during the campaign and Corbyn's grew. It sent the Conservative-supporting tabloids into a bit of a panic. On the eve of the election, the *Daily Mail* dedicated 13 pages to painting Jeremy Corbyn as an 'apologist for terror'. The *Sun*'s 'witty' front page asked the electorate not to 'Chuck Britain in the Cor-Bin', with a picture of the Labour leader peering out from under an actual bin lid. The trouble with this type of personality politics is that parties can rely on style over substance to get themselves elected.

The voting system is unfair

In 2010, there was no clear winner of the general election and we were left with a hung parliament. Lots of haggling between party leaders led the Conservatives and the Liberal Democrats to form a coalition government.

But the deal the Tories did to get the Lib Dems on board was to promise a referendum on the way the UK votes. As we discussed in Chapter 1, our voting system is called first past the post – the candidate who wins the most votes wins the constituency seat, and the first party to get over 50 per cent of the seats wins the election.

There are benefits to this system:

→ It's easy and quick to count the ballots

→ Voters can indicate which party they want to form a government

→ It tends to produce a two-party system so governments don't need support from other parties

→ It encourages parties to be more centrist to appeal to a broad cross-section of voters

But there are negatives to the FPTP system:

→ A candidate wins if they only just squeeze the top spot, even by a handful of votes, while all the votes for the losing candidates are disregarded

→ It can encourage tactical voting, where people vote for the candidate most likely to keep a disliked party from winning their particular seat, rather than voting for the candidate they actually prefer

→ A candidate can win by three votes or 30,000 votes – you could say that in the latter case, most of those thousands of votes are wasted

→ The party that wins the most seats in parliament is not necessarily the party that won the most votes overall

→ Small parties are penalised if their support is spread across the country rather than concentrated in certain areas

The 2015 general election results demonstrated just how unfair this system is to the little guys. The graph opposite shows the average number of votes it took to win each party one seat in parliament, by dividing the amount of votes each party received nationally with the number of seats each party won.

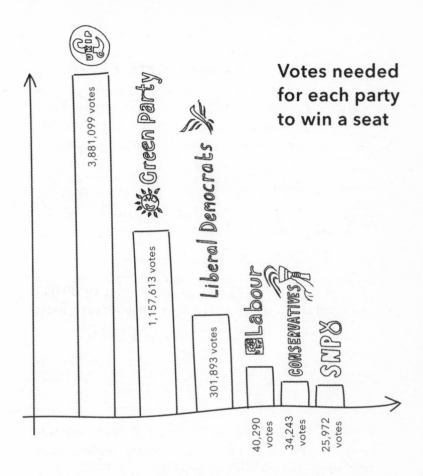

Votes needed for each party to win a seat

- UKIP: 3,881,099 votes
- Green Party: 1,157,613 votes
- Liberal Democrats: 301,893 votes
- Labour: 40,290 votes
- Conservatives: 34,243 votes
- SNP: 25,972 votes

It's unsurprising that the Liberal Democrats wanted to move from the first past the post system to proportional representation, where if a party gains 40 per cent of the national vote that would translate to 40 per cent of the seats. In fact, the Lib Dems were so serious about it that they made a referendum on the voting system their price for agreeing to form a coalition government with the Conservatives in 2015.

The Tories agreed to the deal but they were far from keen. You can see from the graph that they benefit from FPTP, needing fewer votes than Labour and the Lib Dems to win each seat. There are a few different proportional representation voting systems, and the Tories put forward the Alternative Vote method, which is generally seen as the worst of the lot. In fact, Lib Dem leader Nick Clegg had even described it as a 'miserable little compromise' – but it was the only one the Tories were offering. So how does AV work?

In the AV system, you place candidates in order of preference. You can nominate as many preferences as you like, but only the first one is counted initially. A candidate who gets over 50 per cent of the first preferences is elected. If nobody gets 50 per cent of first preferences, the candidate with the fewest first preferences is knocked out. All the ballots that listed the eliminated candidate as the first preference now count the second preferences instead, which get distributed around the remaining candidates. Again, if someone gets past the 50 per cent mark at this point, they're elected. If not, the new candidate at the bottom gets eliminated and the third preferences are distributed – and so on, until either someone gets to 50 per cent or there are no more votes to distribute.

The decision on whether to switch to the AV system was put to a referendum, but the voters rejected the change – 67.9 per cent of those who voted said No, so we stayed with the first past the post system. That time at least, the Tory referendum gamble paid off.

The constituency map can be politically manipulated

There is another plan afoot to shake up the current political landscape and it's called gerrymandering. Every once in a while, the borders of each constituency are redrawn to make sure each one has roughly the same amount of voters. The re-mapping ordered by David Cameron in 2011 will be the biggest since the 1920s, and it's easy to see why it's needed: constituency sizes vary from 20,887 people in Na h-Eileanan an Iar, a Scottish island, to more than 110,000 on the Isle of Wight. The plan includes cutting 50 constituencies altogether – but the problem is that Labour seats bear the brunt of this cull.

The Tories say it's a necessary shake-up to make each vote more equal; the Labour Party see it as gerrymandering, and say the Conservatives are blatantly setting out to make it more likely that they will win a majority in future elections.

The ballot system is stuck in the twentieth century

In an opinion poll taken after the 2015 general election, 65 per cent of people who didn't vote said they would be more likely to if the ballot was somewhere more convenient, such as a supermarket or an office. And almost half of the 18–24-year-olds surveyed said they didn't know how to register their vote or where to find their polling station.

Four out of 10 people said they would be more likely to vote if they could do it online. After all, it's easier to vote on *The X Factor* than it is for a new government. Brazil, Belgium, the Philippines, India and the US have all used e-voting in one form or another. In fact, Estonia introduced it for all its elections in 2005 and now almost a third of its electorate place their ballots via a webpage. But fears that voters could be coerced or bought, or the possibility that an election could be hacked, have put Western democracies off. The battle is not lost: Speaker John Bercow put his political weight behind efforts to find a way to bring safe e-voting to the UK.

There's too much spin in politics

The dark art of spinning has nothing to do with bicycles bolted to the floor and a guy in a tracksuit yelling at you to pedal faster. It's all about putting a certain slant on how you interpret something.

It's the job of a spin-doctor to ensure the media puts a positive slant on their politicians' point of view. SPADS (special advisors to ministers) used to try to remain invisible while painting a positive gloss on events, policies and personalities. The *Telegraph* described them as 'the most shadowy figures in government'. Then New Labour came along in 1997 and Alastair Campbell (Tony Blair's master spinner) became as famous as everyone in the Cabinet – and some would argue even more powerful.

The newspapers embrace spin too – in fact, they take it to another level by shaping editorial direction in favour of their owner's political tastes.

The *Daily Express* was pushing for the UK to vote to leave the EU by printing false stories that the EU wanted to merge the UK and France.

The *Daily Mail* blatantly attacked a High Court ruling on whether the Brexit vote would trigger a constitutional crisis by calling the judges 'enemies of the people'. The headline received more than 1,000 complaints, with critics likening it to 1930s Nazi propaganda.

These are obviously biased headlines that are easy to spot. But it's not always quite so simple to identify what's spun and what's not. It's the same with fake news.

Fake news is everywhere

In the days after the 2016 US presidential election, if you searched for US election results on Google, this story came up top:

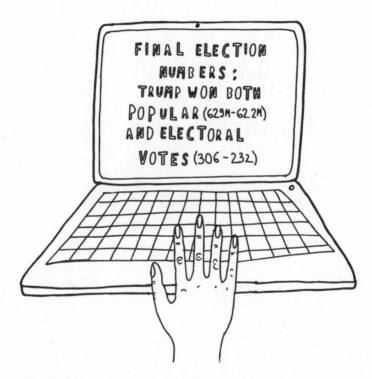

It was fake – the numbers were rubbish. Donald Trump did not win the popular vote. But somehow this false story was the top result on Google.

Just before the presidential election, Donald Trump's campaign adviser Michael Flynn (who would later briefly be his National Security Adviser), had retweeted this:

His tweet suggested that the New York Police Department had found evidence of many crimes committed by Hillary Clinton, including paedophilia. But the story was fake.

The retired general retweeted it to his tens of thousands of followers with the words, 'U decide'. They then retweeted it thousands of times. If the man Trump employed to head National Security couldn't tell the difference between a fake story and a real one, what hope do we have?

We've seen how badly the political system is in need of a makeover. But if you're sitting there thinking, *It's not up to me to fix it*, you're wrong. When you hear or read about something that frustrates or angers you, you have to do something about it. If you wash your hands of the system's problems, nothing will get fixed – you will be left living with politics that don't reflect your views well after today's MPs are long gone.

It's easy to believe that you can't make a difference, but there are incredible stories of what can be achieved when one person takes a stand. The following is an extreme case – people were living in extraordinary circumstances – and in many ways it is a cautionary tale against putting yourself in danger. But it does show how a small act can have a huge impact.

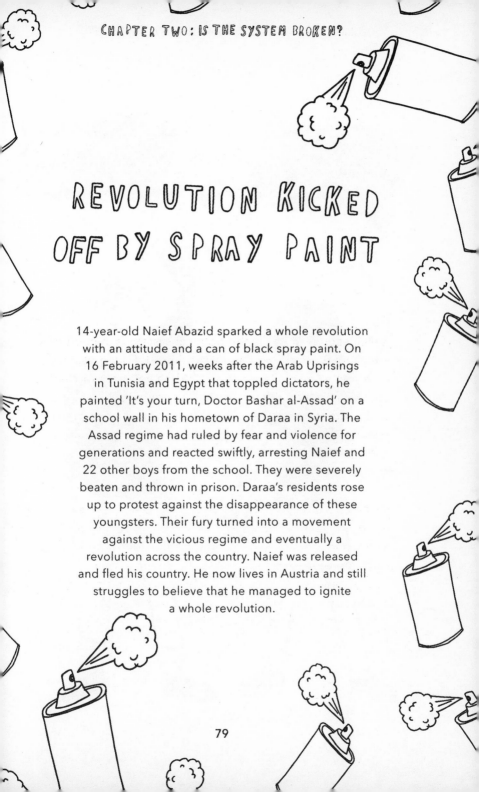

REVOLUTION KICKED OFF BY SPRAY PAINT

14-year-old Naief Abazid sparked a whole revolution with an attitude and a can of black spray paint. On 16 February 2011, weeks after the Arab Uprisings in Tunisia and Egypt that toppled dictators, he painted 'It's your turn, Doctor Bashar al-Assad' on a school wall in his hometown of Daraa in Syria. The Assad regime had ruled by fear and violence for generations and reacted swiftly, arresting Naief and 22 other boys from the school. They were severely beaten and thrown in prison. Daraa's residents rose up to protest against the disappearance of these youngsters. Their fury turned into a movement against the vicious regime and eventually a revolution across the country. Naief was released and fled his country. He now lives in Austria and still struggles to believe that he managed to ignite a whole revolution.

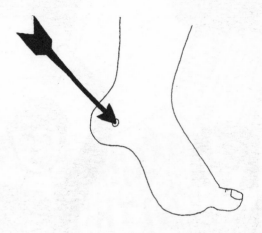

History is littered with stories about how the little guy took on a big business/vicious dictator/ local bully and won.

So if you want to make history, find your opponent's Achilles heel, rally some support and devise a strategy.

CHAPTER THREE: WORKING FROM WITHIN

There's a lot wrong with the current system, but the good news is that there are loads of ways for you to become a voice for change.

But you've got one big decision to make: should you become a Trojan horse – get right into the thick of the political system and push for improvements from within? Or, should you grow your power base from the outside and campaign for a better world by challenging the status quo? Let's start with trying to get things changed from the inside.

Should I join a political party?

You would be a rare breed. In the summer of 2016, just 1.6 per cent of the electorate was a member of one of the three big parties. But it does bring plenty of advantages: being a member of a party means you can go to local meetings and choose your local candidate to stand in the general election. On top of that, you can vote for the leader of your party – that means that if your party wins, you've picked the next prime minister!

We talked earlier about how many politicians don't think about young people much when developing their party's policies. Well, a researcher decided to examine how many times the political party manifestos for the 2015 general election included the term 'young people'.

35

Green Party

30

Labour

21

CONSERVATIVES

11

Liberal Democrats

9

SNP

5

UKIP

For some of the parties, their number of mentions is pretty dismal. But the more young people join a political party, the higher their issues will rise on its agenda – meaning its candidates will start promising to help young people more. It costs less to join a political party than you might think – especially if you're young. As of 2017, here are some of the parties' annual fees:

Conservative Party
£25 standard membership
£5 for under-23-year-olds

Green Party
£38 standard membership
£6 for students

Labour Party
£48 standard membership
£24 for 20–26-year-olds
£3 for 14–19-year-olds and students

Liberal Democrats
£70 standard membership
£1 for first year, then £6 for under-26-year-olds

Scottish National Party
£12 standard membership
£5 for students
£2 for under-15-year-olds

UKIP
£30 standard membership
£2 for under-22-year-olds

There's a party I quite like. But I don't believe in everything it stands for.

I suspect the majority of politicians don't believe in everything their party stands for either. The trick is to pick the party that is closest to your beliefs and then campaign to pull it round to your way of thinking.

However, there is one thing to bear in mind: being a member of a party forces you to take on board its whole agenda and not just the issues you feel strongly about. That means you have to consider what is affecting the whole community. You might be angry at the injustices facing your local LGBT community, but haven't really considered what's making a particular ethnic group angry. You might, with a relative needing surgery, feel that hospital waiting times are far too long – but haven't considered the working hours of junior doctors. Being a member of a party means that everybody's issues have to be taken into account.

Are the smaller parties a waste of effort?

Fringe parties are on the rise. The Green Party, the Scottish National Party and UKIP have all attracted more members in the last few years. But still, with things as they stand at the moment, none of them are likely to get a majority of seats at Westminster and get into power. So is there any point in supporting them?

The UK Independence Party was founded in 1993 with one key objective: to get the UK out of the European Union. The party grew in popularity in the 2010s when some parts of the country became increasingly unhappy about immigration. The party's growth in support saw them win council seats in local government and gain lots of media coverage. They started taking votes in traditionally safe Tory seats – which made the Conservatives sit up and take notice. UKIP succeeded in changing the national conversation: the 2016 referendum on the European Union was called by David Cameron partly due to the anti-EU feeling that UKIP was stirring. Despite the surge in support, UKIP still only won one seat in the 2015 general election, thanks to the FPTP voting system. However, in many ways, that didn't matter. The party got its long-standing wish in June 2016, when the UK voted to pull out of the EU.

The success of UKIP proves that fringe parties can pack a punch on single issues, forcing the national conversation to change. A small – or even non-existent – parliamentary presence doesn't mean they can't have a massive impact. By 2017, UKIP seemed to have run its course – its vote share collapsed by 10.8 points to just 1.8 per cent. The party had achieved its goal: job done.

Should I canvass for a politician?

In the run-up to a general election, candidates recruit a small army of promoters, known as canvassers, to hand out leaflets and knock on doors. Their job is to 'sell' the candidate to the voters. It's a great way for somebody who is thinking about getting into politics to learn how to talk to voters and influence who they will support.

Politics is not an exact science and voters are unpredictable. They even sometimes pick politicians like gamblers at the racecourse pick which horse to back – by how they look. But canvassing will give you a first-hand insight into what matters to people and how your party is doing down on the doorstep.

Should there be youth quotas in parliament?

The British Group Inter-Parliamentary Union, a committee of cross-party MPs and Lords, points out that the average age of British politicians is 50 years old. The group is calling for Parliament to 'harness the power of youth' and is calling for youth quotas in electoral laws. They're arguing for 50 constituency seats to be reserved for MPs aged 18–30.

WOULD THIS GIVE PEOPLE A GREATER VOICE?

→ It might stop other politicians from only thinking about the effect their policies will have during their term in office. Sometimes politicians ignore the longer-term effects of the decisions they make. Younger MPs might be able to keep a check on this, because they would have more at stake in the future

→ Younger MPs may have a fresh outlook on public policy. Decisions about housing or unemployment will affect somebody in their teens differently to somebody in their 50s

→ It would stop older politicians thinking they know best about issues that affect the young. They're not always tuned into what matters to generations other than their own

→ It might bring in new ideas and different ways of doing things – just because something has been done a certain way in the past doesn't mean it's the best way for the future

→ If the opinions of young people are seen to matter in politics, it will help them be seen as equals in other fields too

If you've got a burning ambition to get a seat in parliament, the British Inter-Parliamentary Union may well help you navigate your way in.

How do I stand as a candidate in the general election?

There are a few basics:

You must be **18** years old or above.

You have to be a **BRITISH** or Republic of Ireland citizen, or a citizen of a Commonwealth country and be able to travel freely to the UK.

You need to fill in a **NOMINATION FORM** and get ten signatures. There's a deposit of £500 to enter (you lose this if you don't win at least 5 per cent of the vote).

You'll need an **ELECTION AGENT** who can run your campaign and look after the finances.

You probably won't have much chance standing for one of the big parties (unless you've spent every spare minute of your life until now campaigning for them). But you can stand as an independent candidate or even set up your own political party. Think up a party name – it can't be offensive and must be different from all the other parties. To register your party with the Electoral Commission will cost another £150.

On top of that, to run a good campaign can take quite a bit of money – around £5,000 to £6,000 – and there are specific rules on donations:

> Donors must be British citizens or British-registered companies

> You must send in donation reports to the Electoral Commission so they can see who is funding you

The good news is, you can use the free postal service to let people in your constituency know why you're standing. You can send out one letter or leaflet to all your constituents free of charge – so it had better be good!

As election day draws closer, you'll need to get your supporters out canvassing on your behalf. You're not allowed to pay them, so they'll need to believe in you enough to do it for free.

THE YOUNGEST MEMBER OF PARLIAMENT

Mhairi Black was born in 1994 and elected as the MP for Paisley and Renfrewshire aged 20, making her the 'Baby of the House'. She is the youngest-ever MP (unless you count 13-year-old Christopher Monck who was elected in 1667), proving that you don't have to be a 50-year-old man to speak up for your constituents.

Mhairi had been on Twitter since she was 14 – in fact, she had to delete a few of her 'foul-mouthed' tweets when she decided to get into politics. But social media never lets anything disappear for good – so we know she called Smirnoff Ice the 'drink of gods' and that, as a Partick Thistle supporter, she said she 'fucking hated Celtic'! Getting caught on camera saying she wanted to 'stick the nut on' Labour councillors was, as she said later, not the 'wisest phrase'.

Mhairi, who grew up in Paisley, gave up a job in the Pizza Mario chip shop to concentrate on politics after making some noise during the Scottish referendum debate. She decided the best way to be heard was in Westminster: 'I truly believe that the only way to bring the powers we were promised, and the social justice that Scotland so desperately needs, is to have a strong group of SNP MPs at Westminster to ensure our voices are heard.'

By March 2017, she appeared to have changed her mind, telling the press that she found parliament depressing and defunct: 'It has been nearly two years and I still hate the place. It is depressing ... it's a pain to come up and down every week and you are working with a number of people you find quite troubling.'

You can't say Mhairi's style of politics doesn't get the attention of voters. Her first speech in the Commons has been viewed over 10 million times on YouTube. She's seen as a straight-talking politician that young people identify with.

And it appears that even though she loathes the place, she isn't ready to quit yet. In early 2017, she told the SNP's spring conference that she wasn't going anywhere until the 'job is done' — and by her own admission, that isn't likely to be any time soon. Sometimes, changing the world means gritting your teeth through tough times until your reforms can make a difference.

Can I start smaller and run for a local election?

There are about 18,000 local councillors across England alone who each represent their local community. Their role entails:

→ Representing the ward they were elected in (a ward is like a small constituency)

→ Making and reviewing council policy

→ Scrutinising decisions made by the councillors holding the majority

→ Performing judicial duties

There are two routes to becoming a councillor. You can stand for a political party; to do so you'll need to work locally for that party first to get its support. You can also stand as an independent candidate; you'll need to get to grips with the key issues affecting your area, learn what the council is doing about them and work out how your own opinion differs from the political parties.

You'll need to get 10 local signatures on your nomination papers and submit them 19 working days before election day – then get campaigning!

Remember Roza Salih, the activist who helped set up a campaign for better treatment of asylum seekers when she was in school? In 2017, by then aged 27, she stood as a candidate for the SNP in Glasgow's city council election. Before the vote, she explained why:

❚❚
I am standing to make a change and be a model for others, especially young people and ethnic minorities. No matter where you come from and what your background is, you can make a difference and bring a new perspective to your work. I have always tried to make a difference whatever I have done. Asylum seekers already have so many barriers in front of them when they come over here. I tried to give them hope through education. I am sure there are so many others I can fight for if I am elected. **❚❚**

Roza didn't win a seat on the council in May 2017, but that didn't stop her getting into politics. Ten days after the election, Roza was appointed unopposed to the Scottish Trades Union Congress to represent young people. She's already targeted employers who use zero-hours contracts.

Should I get involved in the Youth Parliament?

The UK Youth Parliament was launched in 1999 and promotes itself as a way for 11–18-year-olds to get into politics. The organisers say, 'It's a way [for young people] to use their elected voice to bring about social change through meaningful representation and campaigning.'

The Youth Parliament has championed the call to bring down the voting age in the UK to 16 years.

To become a member of the Youth Parliament, you have to be elected by other young people in the constituency where you live. Once a year, members of the Youth Parliament sit in the actual House of Commons and debate hot topics. By co-ordinating with schools, the Parliament can draw on a huge electorate. The choice of debate issues in 2016 was decided by almost 1 million young people – that's a lot of opinions. Their top choices were:

- **STOP CUTS** that affect the NHS

- **VOTES AT SIXTEEN** in all elections and referenda

- Make **PUBLIC TRANSPORT** cheaper

- Tackle **RACISM** and religious **DISCRIMINATION**

- Put finance, sex and relationship education and politics on the **SCHOOL CURRICULUM**

But not everyone thinks the Youth Parliament is a good example of democracy. One young student said he had fraudulently voted in the elections for parliamentarians several times via text by using different mobile phones – and that he wasn't the only one. Voters are supposed to be 11–18 years old, but there's no way of checking this. They're also meant to be from the relevant constituency for each candidate – but this is also not properly monitored.

Does the Youth Parliament have a role? Or does it just allow a few hundred pupils to play at being MPs for a day?

Well, at least one of the Youth Parliament's debating issues has hit home. In early 2017, the government announced that all pupils would be taught about safe, healthy relationships and sex in all schools. These classes will include the dangers of sexting, online pornography and sexual harassment. Conversations that address these issues are vital – and the Youth Parliament helped bring them to the attention of the education secretary.

The YP's Votes for 16 campaign has been running for many years, and most political parties now include a commitment to lowering the voting age in their manifestos. The Conservatives and UKIP are the exceptions – but seeing young people tackling important debates in the seat of British democracy may help persuade them that they cannot dodge the age change forever.

100

Taking action

There are many ways at lots of different levels that you could choose to step into the formal structure of politics and change the world.

But to push your own agenda and make your voice heard, you will need to bend the ear of the decision-makers.

That requires some tactical thinking and might even benefit from a little celebrity stardust!

CHANGING MINDS

CHAPTER FOUR: CHANGING MINDS

It may be the politicians who make the decisions, but they are often being influenced by the lobbyists (see Chapter 2).

The lobby groups usually act on behalf of business, charity or trade associations. It is a legitimate way of getting a politician to know the importance of an issue – at least, that's what those who are paying the lobbyists say!

Can I lobby my MP personally?

Definitely – lobbying is not just for corporate bigwigs. Remember those constituency surgeries? Every MP should hold one once a week at their local office. You can go on the politician's website or to the local library to find the surgery hours. MPs face questions on every possible problem or concern, from personal issues about garden fences to local issues like swimming pool opening hours, all the way up to policies on defence and foreign affairs.

The political flavour of your MP might dictate how they respond to your lobby topic. Talking to a Green party politician about promoting recycling, or a Tory MP about reducing crime rates, may be a slam-dunk, but a Labour MP might balk at your call to bring back fox hunting. However, if you're in a marginal seat, you could well get a better reception regardless of your MP's political affiliation. MPs with small majorities value every vote, and cannot afford to back only their own interests.

You could also write to your MP at the House of Commons, email them or call their office and make an appointment to meet them in the Commons. These meetings are more difficult to pin down, but actually turning up at Parliament will show the politician how serious you are about your campaign.

Check out the toolkit in part two for advice on how best to prepare and to shape your argument. MPs are used to debating so you need to be on your A-game!

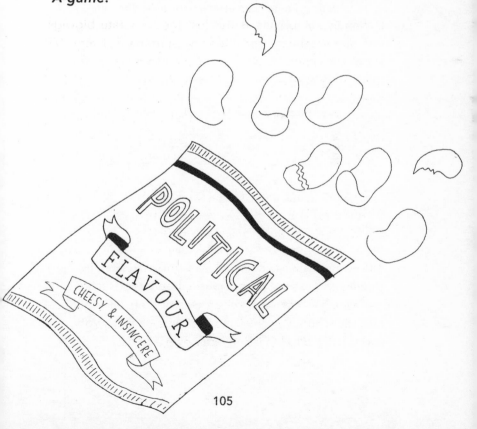

LOBBYING FOR ASYLUM SEEKERS

In 2005, 15-year-old Amal Azzudin started a campaign for a friend and her family who had been taken from their home, detained and threatened with deportation. Amal was determined to help her friend, so she and some of her schoolmates set up a campaign group called the Glasgow Girls to protest about the treatment of asylum seekers. Their message went right to the top of government.

'I was just a normal teenage girl, but when Agnesa was taken, I remember thinking, "I can't just sit down and do nothing. That could have been my family." I thought, "I don't know anything about politics or campaigning, but I have to speak out." There's something in me that can't bear to see wrong. That's the way I was brought up. You speak up for people and fight against what is wrong.

'Agnesa was taken on a Sunday, so on the Monday morning we went to Mr Girvan, our bilingual teacher. I said, "I don't know what we can do, but we need to do something." That's when the other five girls joined in: Emma, Jennifer, Toni-Lee, Ewelina and Roza.

Emma came up with the idea to start a petition and almost everyone in the school signed it, which was amazing. We submitted it to our local MSP [Member of the Scottish Parliament] and he took it to the Scottish Parliament.

'I still remember the day we met the First Minister [Jack McConnell]. There were six of us and him. By that time Agnesa had been saved, but she had explained how she was treated, seeing her father locked up in a detention centre, which is basically a jail. She said they did counts each night to check everyone was in their rooms and every door was locked. It was horrible.

'Getting things changed by lobbying politicians is not the only way. But there's a reason why there are politicians. In our case, going to the Scottish Parliament was great. We had cross-party support across the parliament.

'We still keep in touch with Jack McConnell. He's a Lord now, so when I come to London I text him and he says, "Come have a cup of tea in the House of Lords".'

Are trade unions effective lobbyists?

Trade unions are organisations that aim to protect the workers or employees they represent. They are independent of the employer and can negotiate conditions and pay on the employees' behalf.

But if statistics are anything to go by, young people are just not interested in joining a trade union. In 2015, almost 40 per cent of trade union members were aged over 50, while just 5 per cent of members were aged 16 to 24. Young people seem to be bucking the national trend, because between 2012 and 2014, an extra 54,000 older people signed up to one union or another.

SO WHAT IS IT THAT'S TURNING YOUNG PEOPLE OFF THE UNIONS?

After all, they're groups set up to campaign to make work a better place. But trade unions are not as powerful as they once were. Employers nowadays often refuse to recognise trade unions so it can be difficult for employees to have a group voice. Some employees also fear that joining a union could blot your record in many private companies, although in most cases it is illegal for companies to treat people badly because they belong to a union.

In fact, some argue that trade unions are an out-of-date concept, which is why young people are less interested. After all, lots of young people don't identify with having a trade, don't work for just one employer and don't expect to be in the same job all their life.

Most young people are more likely to turn to Google with a work issue than to contact a trade union – which explains why some bright coding sparks are working to replace the union rep with a handy app. One former call-centre employee who wasn't happy with his working conditions quit and set up the FairOffice app. It allows employees to put suggestions to their boss anonymously. The idea is that it provokes a conversation without the boss ever knowing which employee stuck their neck out.

But if trade unions disappear, you might miss them more than you'd expect. Watching the news today, you'd be forgiven for thinking that all the unions do is promote the Labour Party and go on marches.

Celebrities from comedians, actors, celebrities and even magicians have used their platforms to be vocal about politics.

Doctor Who actor David Tennant has recorded several party political broadcasts for the Labour Party over the years.

Take That star Gary Barlow backed Conservative David Cameron with the line, 'There's no one more with-it than Dave'.

Radiohead frontman Thom Yorke has regularly sung out for the Green Party.

Snooker superstar Ronnie O'Sullivan played a few frames with then-Labour leader Ed Miliband.

Pop star Lily Allen has been a staunch supporter of Jeremy Corbyn since 2016.

Rapper Tinie Tempah is supposedly best mates with Labour MP Chuka Umunna, and has said he'd make a good future Labour leader.

Sean Connery spoke in glowing terms about Scottish National Party leader Nicola Sturgeon.

Harry Potter star Daniel Radcliffe caused a stir when he made a public switch from Lib Dem to Labour.

Simon Cowell once said David Cameron had the 'substance and stomach' to lead the country in tricky times.

In many cases, celebrities make poor political advisors. But there are some who get it right – who put their names to a cause, spend time visiting those in trouble or join campaigns that aren't getting the attention they deserve. The royal trio of William, Kate and Harry chose to campaign for a better understanding of mental illness, an issue that was often swept under the carpet until they made some noise.

Angelina Jolie has been on field missions all over the world, raising awareness of the plight of refugees and internally displaced people in more than 20 countries. Even Thor can get political. Actor Chris Hemsworth started campaigning for greater environmental protection after going on holiday to the Maldives and seeing how plastic is impacting on our oceans.

Celebrities campaigning on specific issues are often more persuasive than those who support a particular political party.

I asked legendary CHANNEL FOUR anchorman JON SNOW what he thought of famous faces getting involved in politics.

" *My sense is that celebrity endorsements of conventional political parties tend to have little influence. I don't perceive any great effect from them in the past. However, there is some evidence that fringe parties can benefit from such endorsements at least to get themselves 'on the map'.*

The Green Party and other fringe parties have benefitted from celebrity sponsors in the past. The classic example is Glenda Jackson for Labour. A great actress, but never a great politician. **"**

Glenda Jackson won two Oscars before moving on to actually becoming an MP for the Labour Party in 1992. She was told she was replacing one form of theatre for another, but remarked,

" *If that was the case, the Commons is remarkably under-rehearsed, the lighting is appalling and acoustic is even worse.* **"**

She caused controversy in a speech in 2013, two days after the death of Margaret Thatcher, when she attacked the former Prime Minister for greed, selfishness, not caring for the weak and doing 'extraordinary human damage'. It was met with cries of 'Shame on you' from MPs on the other side of the chamber and got 1.6 million views on YouTube. Jackson left politics two years later.

Speaking up

Westminster is slowly becoming more representative of all aspects of British society, but there's still plenty of work to be done. The old-school British political system is struggling to know how to engage younger voters, so your involvement could be warmly welcomed.

You're up to speed on how to make some noise inside the system. You know how to put your foot on the political ladder and how to get yourself a face-to-face meeting with the decision-makers.

Who better to help modernise our great democratic system of government?

But going down the traditional route is far from the only way to make a difference. There has never before been such a huge opportunity to get your voice heard from outside the walls of Westminister. More and more campaigns are emerging on the outside, forcing the establishment to pay attention.

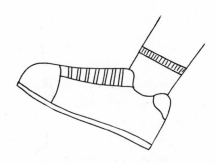

CHAPTER FIVE :
STEP OUTSIDE THE SYSTEM

We've talked about how you can make your voice heard within the political system. But if the system IS the problem, why try to work inside it at all?

Some of the traditional ways can be too slow and too quiet to drive real change. So if you're inspired to stand up and shout, this is the chapter for you. And there are plenty of ways to change the world – from the outside.

Petitions

Starting a petition, or signing one that's already underway, is a relatively gentle way to make some noise. Petitions show the decision-makers that there are lots of people who feel passionate about an issue. According to the campaigning website change.org, Brits are more keen to sign petitions than almost any other citizens in the world. Gathering a petition used to be a question of printing off reams of paper and thrusting them under people's noses to sign. Today you can still do that if you really want, but doing it online is much easier – and social networks help get you in front of loads more people.

There are a few things to bear in mind when deciding if a petition is the best way to go:

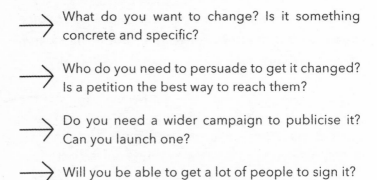

What do you want to change? Is it something concrete and specific?

Who do you need to persuade to get it changed? Is a petition the best way to reach them?

Do you need a wider campaign to publicise it? Can you launch one?

Will you be able to get a lot of people to sign it?

Once you've settled on a petition, the wording you use is important if you want to maximise how many people sign up.

1) Keep it SIMPLE and to the point.

2) BACK UP your demand with information that supports the need for change.

3) Don't make it too FORMAL

4) Ask the people signing it to include PERSONAL PROOF of their existence, such as postcodes or email addresses.

5) Use SOCIAL MEDIA to reach as many people as possible.

6) DELEGATE responsibility for collecting signatures if you can.

7) Include a DEADLINE by which all signatures should be collected and the petition will be handed in.

There are lots of websites that you can use to start a petition, such as avaaz.org and 38degrees.org.uk. If you're targeting the government, use its official petitions site https://petition.parliament.uk. If you get 10,000 signatures, the government has to respond to it. Get 100,000 and they'll consider a debate in Parliament.

PETITION SPECIALIST JEREMY HEIMANS

Jeremy Heimans was born to be a campaigner. By the age of seven, this young Australian was handing out his own political leaflets to parents at his primary school. By the age of 12 he had won a peace prize, represented Australia at a European conference and met the prime minister. It wasn't long before he moved to the US to become what he calls a 'Movement Entrepreneur'. Jeremy set up Avaaz.org – an online platform offering petitions and other forms of direct action. It now mobilises millions of members.

'I was a serious kid who was also very political. I am the child of two immigrants, one a Holocaust survivor, so I always felt connected to questions of injustice and otherness. It was pro-immigration leaflets that I wrote myself that I was handing out at age seven – the first thing I can remember doing politically.

'I think it's important that people take action not just on the issues that one has direct experience of, but also to express solidarity with other people who may also be suffering, even when the experience is different. I'd encourage young people to make sure they're doing a mix of things that feel personally resonant and that are an expression of solidarity.

'Social media is making campaigns much less top-down. But don't assume the tools themselves will do the work – tech alone isn't the answer. It can be a useful way to meet people where they are when trying to mobilise them around any particular issue.

'Challenge yourself to think about where the audiences might already be (such as new messenger apps or video platforms) and think of creative ways to connect with them there.'

Petitions can be incredibly effective – they raise awareness of issues, put pressure on politicians and organisations, and allow people to take action without committing a lot of their time. Sometimes they can mean the difference between freedom and captivity for someone.

RELEASING IRANIAN PROTESTOR

Ghoncheh Ghavami, a 26-year-old British-Iranian woman, had joined a demonstration in Tehran, Iran calling for women to be allowed to watch a volleyball match when she was arrested. Her brother Iman, who lives in London, launched a campaign to get her freed and set up a petition. It was signed by more than 777,000 people and Ghoncheh was released.

Iman thinks the petition played a pivotal role in putting pressure on Iran's politicians.

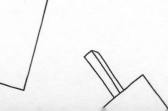
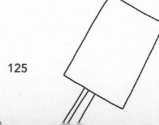

Petitions don't always work though. Sometimes, a petition with vast amounts of support still doesn't manage to force change. For example, in 2016, there was a huge reaction when one man won an election: Mr Donald Trump.

When Prime Minister Theresa May visited President Trump shortly after his election, she invited him to come for a full state visit to the UK. That means he'd get to go to Buckingham Palace to eat scones and drink tea with the Queen. Mr Trump's language and policies have upset a lot of people in the UK, so this invitation angered them. An online petition was set up calling on the government to withdraw the invitation because it would cause embarrassment for the Queen. At one point it was being signed by a thousand people a minute. It didn't just reach the 100,000 signatures needed for a debate to be considered in parliament – it passed the 1.8 MILLION mark. So as a petition it did its job, prompting a lively debate in the Commons lasting almost three hours. But the Prime Minister had made it clear that staying friendly with the UK's most powerful ally was more important than stopping a visit that almost 2 million people were against.

Letter campaigns

Flooding the letterbox of a decision-maker is another way of waking them up to a popular point of view. Letter campaigns are a bit like petitions because they rely on volume to make an impact, but they can cause more of a disturbance – whether by way of heavy postbags dumped on the doormat or emails swamping an inbox. It also means that each activist has an opportunity to talk personally about why the issue matters to them, if they want to.

If you have a clear target for your campaign, a mass mail drop can really make your point. There are a few tips to help you ensure maximum impact:

MAKE YOUR GOAL CLEAR

SHARE YOUR CAMPAIGN ON SOCIAL MEDIA

for the greatest reach

PROVIDE TEMPLATES FOR THE LETTER

featuring key points to include. This will make it easier for other people to join in and will make it clear that all the letters are from the same campaign

Of course, you don't have to set up your own letter-writing campaign – being one of the letter-writers makes a huge difference too. Amnesty International has taken mass letter-writing to another level. This global movement targeting human rights abuses has over 4.6 million people onside – an enormous grassroots campaigning resource.

In 2009, Amnesty launched its 'Write for Rights' campaign, asking people to write letters of protest when somebody's basic human rights were being attacked. And these letters have often made a huge difference.

LIFE SENTENCE

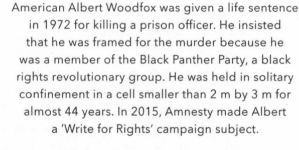

American Albert Woodfox was given a life sentence in 1972 for killing a prison officer. He insisted that he was framed for the murder because he was a member of the Black Panther Party, a black rights revolutionary group. He was held in solitary confinement in a cell smaller than 2 m by 3 m for almost 44 years. In 2015, Amnesty made Albert a 'Write for Rights' campaign subject.

More than 200,000 people took action by writing letters of protest, and in 2016 Albert walked out of that cell as a free man.

Protest art

Art, music, poetry and the spoken word have all been used to send some of the world's most powerful protest messages. These media can often cross languages, cultures and religions, uniting people behind a common cause without the need to say anything more. A powerful artistic message can send your protest viral, and if you think creatively, it's a great way to express yourself.

Ai Weiwei has used his art to address the corruption and human rights abuses of the Chinese government. In one campaign he took photographs of his middle finger sticking up at various monuments including Tiananmen Square in Beijing – the scene of a student-led democracy protest in 1989 that was brutally put down by the army killing hundreds of protesters.

Russian feminist punk rock group Pussy Riot made global headlines in 2012 when they burst into one of Moscow's leading Orthodox cathedrals to sing a 'punk prayer' against the oppressive regime of President Putin. It landed its members a jail sentence but also an international following.

Marches

Campaigners have been staging demonstrations to bring about change for centuries. In fact, the word 'demonstration' was first used in the mid-1800s. Back then it was also called a 'monster meeting' – a great term! Protest marches are fantastic for capturing media attention, and they're one of the most effective ways of attracting the notice of decision-makers. However, they do require some planning.

First of all, alert the authorities. By law, in the UK you have to let the police know some details about your march, so that they can plan how it might affect the neighbourhood and take any necessary precautions. It's best to give the local police the following information in writing six days before you intend to march:

→ DATE AND TIME OF THE MARCH

→ THE ROUTE YOU INTEND TO TAKE

→ NAMES AND ADDRESSES OF THE ORGANISERS

The police should try to accommodate your requests, but they may ask you to change your route, limit how long it lasts and put a cap on the numbers.

GAY PRIDE

The first gay march in the UK took place when 150 men walked together through Highbury Fields in London in the autumn of 1970. This grew into Gay Pride two years later, attracting 2,000 supporters. But in 1988, a controversial new law was introduced, and the popularity of the Gay Pride march exploded. Section 28 made it illegal to promote gay relationships as acceptable in schools. Campaigners fought against this law for 15 years, when it was eventually thrown out – but during that period, Gay Pride became Pride London. By 2012, the LGBTQ community in London formed a company to take over what had grown into a festival and parade that attracts tens of thousands of people each year. This protest movement helped to change the way people think of the LGBTQ community.

However, like petitions, garnering huge numbers for a protest doesn't automatically mean that change will occur.

BIGGEST PROTEST IN HISTORY

The largest protest event in history took place against a coalition of Western nations going to war in Iraq. On 15 February 2003, more than 600 cities around the world held demonstrations. In the UK, hundreds of thousands of people from 250 cities and towns took to the streets of London – organisers put the number of protestors at 2 million – marching 5.6 km into Hyde Park. Around the world, between 6 and 11 million people protested over that weekend. One newspaper described the situation as, 'Two superpowers on the planet – the United States, and worldwide public opinion'. But in the end, the world's biggest protest failed to stop the war. Troops went to Iraq and the war's aftermath continues today.

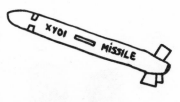

WOMEN'S MARCH

Retired lawyer and grandmother Teresa Shook, who lives in Hawaii, was so depressed that Donald Trump had won the US presidency that she decided to create a Facebook event calling for a march after Trump's inauguration. She was happy to see she'd got 40 responses before she headed to bed that night. She woke up the next morning to more than 10,000 replies on her page. That is how the Women's March on 21 January 2017 got going. It became the largest single-day demonstration in US history and prompted a worldwide protest about much more than Donald Trump. As well as women's rights, people carried placards for immigration and healthcare reform, LGBTQ rights, racial equality, workers' rights and many other causes.

The march filled many people with hope. However, the big question the next day was: How could this solidarity be channelled into positive change?

Capitalising on the energy generated by a protest march is very important if you are going to build that support into a campaign. It's easy to believe you have achieved momentum that will keep growing, but once the march is over, your work has only just begun. You need to start getting organised:

→ Set up a database of the people who turned up

→ Organise communications with activists from similar groups so you can share databases of supporters who have agreed to be kept in the loop

→ Link everyone together on social media

→ Devise a calendar of similar events

The organisers of the Women's March in the US set up Next Up Huddles, community gatherings that brought together activists tackling a range of issues including civil rights and healthcare. People can enter their zip code on the campaign website to learn about events being organised in their area.

Did you go on the Women's March? Do you know others who went along too? Have you been involved in a follow-up meeting to keep the momentum going? If not, why not launch your own?

Direct protest

You could take your protest directly to the politicians. Brian Haw did just that. He led a one-man protest in Parliament Square against the war in Iraq for 10 years. The authorities tried to get him removed but he stood firm, demonstrating our democratic right to protest — even right in front of the Houses of Parliament.

He's one of many people throughout history who decided that the best way to get their voice heard was to direct it straight at the decision-makers.

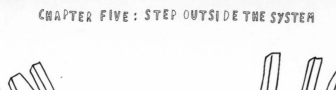

VOTES FOR WOMEN

Imagine you're a young woman growing up in the 1890s and the guys you grew up with get to vote — but you're not allowed to. You hear about a group of women making some noise about this injustice, so you find out where they're meeting and go along. There are only a few of you, but you're sure others in different parts of the country feel the same way.

That is how the suffragist movement started and it's why women can vote today.

They didn't win the right overnight. It took lots of individual groups getting up all over the country and campaigning for a change. By 1903, Emmeline Pankhurst and her daughters Sylvia, Christabel and Adela were unhappy that this growing movement of angry women was not making real progress, so they set up the Women's Social and Political Union. These suffragettes were different — they were prepared to get violent. In 1905, Christabel and Annie Kenney went to a meeting in Manchester where Liberal politicians Winston Churchill and Sir Edward Grey were speaking. The women interrupted — shouting,

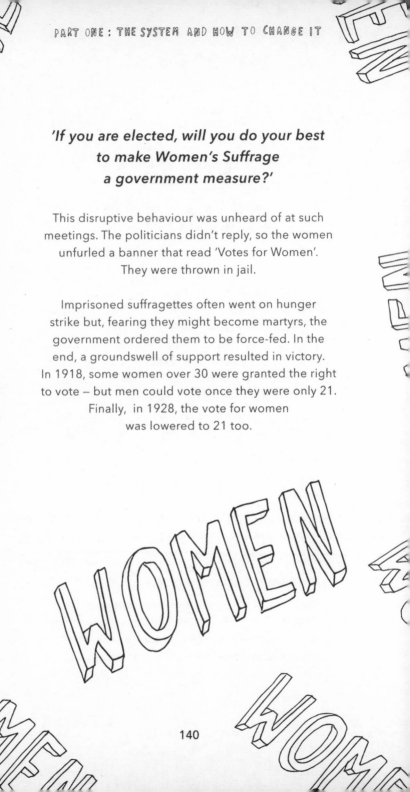

*'If you are elected, will you do your best
to make Women's Suffrage
a government measure?'*

This disruptive behaviour was unheard of at such
meetings. The politicians didn't reply, so the women
unfurled a banner that read 'Votes for Women'.
They were thrown in jail.

Imprisoned suffragettes often went on hunger
strike but, fearing they might become martyrs, the
government ordered them to be force-fed. In the
end, a groundswell of support resulted in victory.
In 1918, some women over 30 were granted the right
to vote – but men could vote once they were only 21.
Finally, in 1928, the vote for women
was lowered to 21 too.

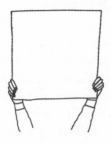

Sit-ins

Sometimes, disrupting the status quo by occupying somewhere is the best way to make your point. The sit-in usually lasts for a set period of time, or until the decision-makers agree to your demand.

The Arab Uprisings in 2011 used occupation to great effect. Protestors against the Egyptian regime refused to leave Tahrir Square in central Cairo, a movement that eventually toppled a dictator.

And the Occupy Wall Street movement in New York inspired Occupy protests all over the world in solidarity against social inequality.

GREENSBORO SIT-IN

Perhaps the most famous sit-in protest took place in 1960 in Greenboro, North Carolina, USA. It was 1 February and four African-American students at an all-black college headed to a department store named Woolworth's. They were allowed into the main shopping area, but the attached restaurant was for whites only. The boys decided it was time to make a change, so they planned a protest.

On 1 February, they walked into the restaurant and asked for food.They were refused by the white waitress, who pointed to the other side of the counter, where there was no seating, saying, 'Negroes get food at the other end'. The waitress asked the students to leave, but instead they sat down. The restaurant shut 30 minutes later, so it was only a brief sit-in – but when the students got back to campus, news of their stand had reached their peers. The next day, 24 men staged the same sit-in. A white woman turned up for lunch but walked out when she saw the black men sitting there. By 4 February, white female students from another college had joined the sit-in.

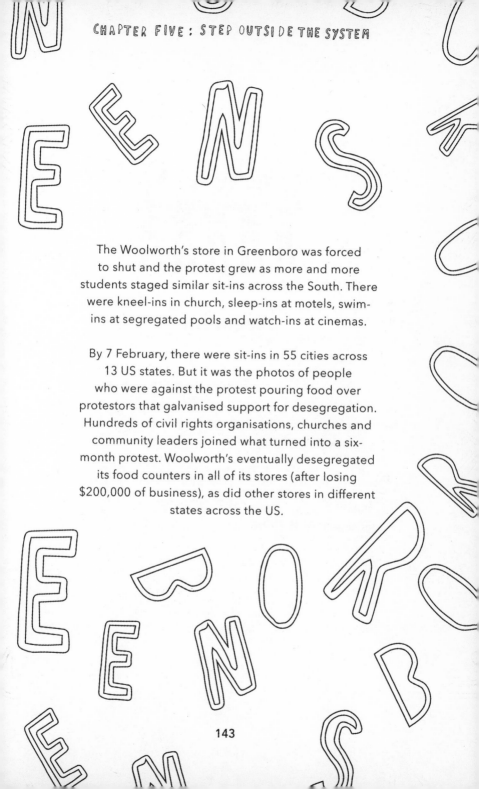

The Woolworth's store in Greenboro was forced to shut and the protest grew as more and more students staged similar sit-ins across the South. There were kneel-ins in church, sleep-ins at motels, swim-ins at segregated pools and watch-ins at cinemas.

By 7 February, there were sit-ins in 55 cities across 13 US states. But it was the photos of people who were against the protest pouring food over protestors that galvanised support for desegregation. Hundreds of civil rights organisations, churches and community leaders joined what turned into a six-month protest. Woolworth's eventually desegregated its food counters in all of its stores (after losing $200,000 of business), as did other stores in different states across the US.

Picketing

If your issue is workplace-related, you might decide to go on strike and stage a picket line. This involves standing outside your place of work, telling others why you're striking and why they should stop working too.

However, bear in mind that it's illegal to prevent other people from doing their usual work or to be abusive towards them.

MINERS' STRIKE

The 1984-5 miners' strike was a reaction to the coal industry's attempt to close mines in Britain. The key characters were Prime Minister Margaret Thatcher and head of the National Union of Mineworkers (NUM), Arthur Scargill. At its peak, the strike by the miners involved 142,000 workers. To try to persuade miners who didn't agree with the strike from going to work, the NUM set up picket lines. But because there hadn't been a national vote on the strike, the police were often sent to break up the picket lines. In the end, the government starved the miners into submission.

Most striking miners eventually ran out of money and the redundancy packages being offered by their employers were their only way out. The strike failed; in 1983, Britain had 174 working pits. In 2015, the country's last deep pit was closed.

DAGENHAM LADIES

A strike started by five female sewing machinists in Dagenham led to a massive leap forwards in equal pay for women in 1968. The women worked for the Ford Motor Company and were angry that their sewing jobs were considered less skilled than similar roles being performed by men in production. They decided to go on strike and stopped making car seat covers – a move that eventually brought a halt to all car production at the plant.

The Secretary of State for Employment and Productivity was Barbara Castle, who heard their call for equality and helped negotiate a pay increase – but it was still 8 per cent below the men's. The strike sparked a parliamentary debate and led to Castle drawing up the Equal Pay Act of 1970.

Organising protests

You might like to consider these questions before you put out the call to get people to turn out for your march, direct protest or occupation:

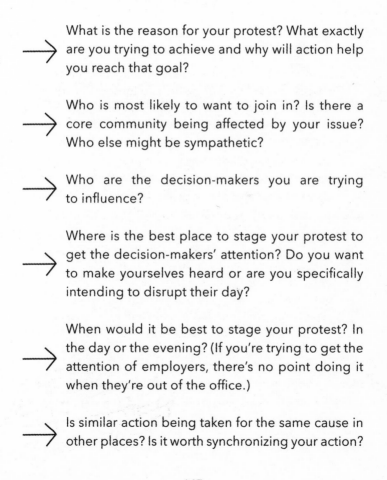

What is the reason for your protest? What exactly are you trying to achieve and why will action help you reach that goal?

Who is most likely to want to join in? Is there a core community being affected by your issue? Who else might be sympathetic?

Who are the decision-makers you are trying to influence?

Where is the best place to stage your protest to get the decision-makers' attention? Do you want to make yourselves heard or are you specifically intending to disrupt their day?

When would it be best to stage your protest? In the day or the evening? (If you're trying to get the attention of employers, there's no point doing it when they're out of the office.)

Is similar action being taken for the same cause in other places? Is it worth synchronizing your action?

Volunteering

There's another way that you can change the status quo without getting involved in protesting. If you see a bad situation, why not roll your sleeves up and get to work improving it? You can make a difference by supporting the elderly, cleaning up local parks, working for an animal charity or staffing a food bank.

There are a whole host of ways to get involved in your own community, and it's a great way to learn how to engage with local people. Visit sites like do-it.org and volunteeringmatters.org.uk, where you can put in your postcode and get a list of opportunities in your area to volunteer for.

Alternatively, if you're passionate about issues further afield, you could take a gap year or volunteer during time off school or work to travel abroad. Groups like Global Vision International (gvi.co.uk) can help you make a difference in many countries worldwide. If there's something going on that you don't like, work to change it.

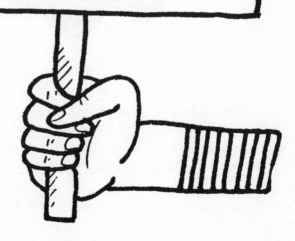

Standing up to the system

If you're keen to get out and at 'em, you now have the basics on marching, petitioning, picketing, protesting and occupation.

You have seen how your activist brothers and sisters took to the streets and got things changed. Now it's time to take your campaign methods to another level.

The masses are taking on the establishment like never before, with campaigns emerging in new ways and huge protests challenging the status quo. But masterminding a campaign requires a certain skillset.

This toolkit is here to help.

A TOOLKIT FOR CHANGE

The activist's toolkit is a bunch of skills you need to collect if you're going to get on with changing the world:

KNOW the law

SPOT the bias

BREAK OUT of your comfort zone

DETECT fake news

TRACK breaking news

GET your message out

CREATE your story

CONQUER social media

SPEAK loud and proud

CRACK debating

AVOID the hypnotists

EMBRACE your specialist knowledge

There is no single right way to design a campaign, but there are some common pitfalls to avoid and great methods to consider. With these tools firmly in your head, you can accelerate your progress and magnify your impact.

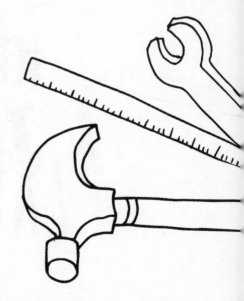

TOOL ONE: KNOW THE LAW

Before we decide what we want to make some noise about, we need to learn some rules.

It's a bit like being on a football pitch and being careful to stay onside – otherwise your goal won't count. You don't want to fall foul of the activists' rulebook either. So, first, learn the rules of the game. You might decide to break them later (sometimes a bit of civil disobedience goes a long way), but it's best to know if you are stepping over the line before you do it.

Free speech

We live in a democracy, so that means we are entitled to the glorious principle called freedom of speech. It's a right that people in other parts of the world fight and die for. So if you're unhappy about something, you have every right to speak up.

However, that doesn't mean you can say anything you want. Even democracies have to impose limits on what you're allowed to say and what you are not.

In 1951, the UK ratified the European Convention of Human Rights, making it the law that we're all allowed to express ourselves. However, the Convention lists many exceptions to the idea of free expression, making it illegal to use threatening or abusive language, or speech that's likely to cause a 'breach of the peace'. That sort of speech is often called 'hate speech'. The European Union describes hate speech as 'expression which spreads, incites, promotes or justifies ... hatred based on intolerance.'

There's another law, too – Article 19 of the International Covenant on Civil and Political Rights, which was signed by the democratic countries in the United Nations. It states that freedom of expression should be limited so that it gives 'respect for the rights and reputations of others, and protection of national security, public order, public health or morals'.

So there are limits, which makes sense. But sometimes it's not clear what's allowed and what isn't. In fact, courts have made rulings that seem to allow all sorts of hate speech.

WILDERS AND RACIAL HATRED

Dutch right-wing MP Geert Wilders called for a ban on the Qur'an. He was put on trial in 2009 for stoking up racial hatred and discrimination because he compared the Qur'an to Hitler's book *Mein Kampf*. The court ruled that Wilders' comments had been 'acceptable within the context of public debate'.

Verdict – not guilty

GERMANY POSTERGATE

The far-right Nationaldemokratische Partei Deutschland was ordered to remove a poster during elections in Berlin in 2011. The poster's slogan was 'Step on the gas!' The opposition complained that this was a direct reference to the Holocaust, when the Nazis massacred millions of Jewish people by putting them in gas chambers. Another posted had a cartoon of people who looked like immigrants on a magic carpet with a slogan wishing them a 'Safe flight home'. The Berlin State Court ruled that the posters were within the freedom of speech laws.

Verdict – not guilty

MASS MURDER IN ATTACK AGAINST CARTOONISTS

The French satirical magazine *Charlie Hebdo* is known for routinely publishing caricatures of the Prophet Muhammad, as well as Catholics, Jews and politicians. But in 2006, it was a cartoon depicting a sobbing Prophet Muhammad under the headline 'Muhammad overwhelmed by fundamentalists' that really upset the Muslim world. The Great Mosque of Paris and the Union of Islamic Organisations of France took the magazine to court, but the ruling was in favour of freedom of expression. *Charlie Hebdo* saw this as a green light to keep ridiculing the faith of Islam.

→ 2007 front page headline: '*Charlie Hebdo* must be veiled!'

→ 2011 headline: '100 lashes if you don't die of laughter'. The prophet was named as the guest editor of that edition. *Charlie Hebdo*'s offices were fire-bombed shortly after the edition was published.

→ Later in 2011 and 2012: cartoons on the magazine's website depict a Muslim man as gay and naked.

→ 2013 65-page special edition: featured an illustrated biography of the prophet.

At 11.30 one Paris morning in 2015, the weekly editorial meeting was in full swing at *Charlie Hebdo*. Corinne Rey, a cartoonist, had just picked up her daughter from day care and was walking into the building when two masked men armed with Kalashnikovs forced her to enter the code for the magazine's offices. They burst into the conference room and opened fire, killing the editor and his bodyguard, four cartoonists, three other editorial staff and a guest. The terrorists' excuse for this attack was words and cartoons.

By law, freedom of speech is supposed to be limited if it's going to provoke violence. However, this is more complicated than it sounds. Some people say that Muslims regard the Prophet Muhammad as a model of virtue and dignity, so using his image as an object of satire is unacceptable. But others argue that free speech relates to every religion and that no subject should be off limits. Whatever your opinion, all right-minded people believe there is never justification for barbaric attacks like the one on *Charlie Hebdo*.

We need to speak responsibly and recognise the limits of free speech.

But we also need to be on our guard for decision-makers who attempt to curtail this freedom in their own interests. Democracy works on the premise that opposing ideas are aired and debated. If the powerful refuse to acknowledge viewpoints opposing their own, democracy is failing. Silencing the opposition is not unusual in dictatorships: President Abdel Fattah al-Sisi of Egypt and President Robert Mugabe of Zimbabwe are masters at this practice.

US president Herbert Hoover summed it up this way:

EACH DICTATOR HAS SUPPRESSED ALL FREE SPEECH EXCEPT HIS OWN

But the American president, often referred to as the leader of the free world, is expected to embrace political debate and discourse. The current incumbent in the White House is sending a chill wind to rustle the pages of the American Bill of Rights. President Trump has said he wants to 'open up' libel laws to punish journalists who write 'mean' things about him, he has fired people who disagree with him and he's revoked access from press outlets that criticise his presidency. Free speech is under threat in one of the world's most established democracies, and it's up to all of us to protect it.

Freedom of assembly

This sounds a bit like there's a law to let you have a party, but it's more about giving you the right to meet others, discuss issues and have opinions – such as at protests, public meetings and marches.

CLASHES WITH THE EDL

In 2010, the English Defence League (a far-right protest movement) was planning a protest in Bradford – so the Unite Against Fascism group organised a counter-protest at the same place. Local people feared that these two groups would clash, so they appealed to the police to stop the EDL protest. The police said that unless there was evidence that violence was planned, they had to let the protests go ahead: it's the law. There were clashes, but only between the EDL and the police, who managed to keep the two protest groups well away from each other.

Freedom of information

A new law was introduced in 2000 that gave people the right to access official records. If you put in a request for information from a public authority, it has to tell you if they have the information – and, if so, they have to give it to you.

There are exceptions. For example, you can't access court records or information that relates to security matters. But generally speaking, the authority needs a good reason not to let you find what you're looking for. When it comes to activism, digging for information can strengthen your cause.

So how do you stay within the law?

If you know the legal boundaries then you won't get into trouble by crossing them. So remember, you are:

FREE

→ to shock, disturb or offend

→ to request information from a publicly funded body

→ to march, demonstrate, stage sit-ins, form trade unions and organise meetings

→ to refuse to join an association

NOT FREE

→ to speak if it causes violence, hatred and discrimination

→ to encourage violent protest

→ to send a grossly offensive, obscene or menacing message by social media or email

→ to stir up religious hatred or hatred of someone's sexual orientation

→ to get sensitive information from intelligence agencies or court records

→ to organise or take part in violent confrontations

→ to encourage and glorify terrorism – it's illegal under anti-terrorism laws

TOOL TWO : SPOT THE BIAS

Every activist worth his or her salt needs to be sure of their facts.

You can't expect to persuade people to join your campaign or sign your petition if you've based it on fake, false and flippant facts. But it's not easy working out which are the reliable sources and which are full of shit.

The first question we need to ask is who can we trust. Let's start with the old-fashioned news outlets: newspapers, magazines and news channels that have been publishing facts for decades and employ experienced journalists to thoroughly check their stories before publishing or broadcasting.

However, as we've already learned, most of these outlets have a bias. Their editors steer the coverage to reflect the owner's politics. We need to know what slant they put on their stories and how they do it. There are a number of ways:

→ The point of view the story is given

→ The use of inflammatory or one-sided language used about a subject

→ The prominence of the story in the broadcast or paper

→ The number of stories about the same topic

After the Brexit referendum, a website was set up to monitor the stories that newspapers were printing. Infacts.org fact-checked them all and found that many papers were playing fast and loose with the truth. One of the most likely topics for bullshit replacing facts was that of migrants. The *Daily Mail*, *Mail Online*, *Daily Express*, *Daily Telegraph* and *Sun* all published false stories to boost the Leave campaign.

But the *Telegraph* was being dishonest about the figures. It had added the number of short-term EU visitors over the previous five years to the Office of National Statistics' estimate of long-term migrants.

The *Sun* was also being untruthful. The four in five statistic wasn't based on the total number of jobs. It was the figure for the number of *new* jobs if you discounted everyone who had changed jobs, retired or stopped working. The London School of Economics put the actual number of people not born in the UK to be hired at 17.5 per cent, a figure which also includes UK nationals who were born abroad — so the *Sun* was way off the mark.

So we can't always trust the old-school newspapers and their websites to give us information straight. The best you can do is read articles from both sides of the political divide.

This is the political position the national newspapers take:

LEFT CENTRE RIGHT

CENTRE LEFT

CENTRE RIGHT

i News

Morning Star

The Financial Times

Independent

Daily Mail/Mail on Sunday

Sun

Daily Star

Daily Express

Guardian/ Observer

Mirror/ Sunday Mirror

Daily Telegraph

The Times/ The Sunday Times

A poll conducted across Europe in 2016 found that more people in the UK thought their media was too right-wing than in any other country.

So when you're reading a story in one of these newspapers, you need to keep questioning whether the reporting is biased. Ask yourself 'Is this exaggerated?', 'Do I trust the way this is written?' and 'Are the facts and figures reliable?'

It's the same with TV news channels, websites, Twitter feeds and blogs. Whatever we are reading, watching or listening to, we always need to question the source.

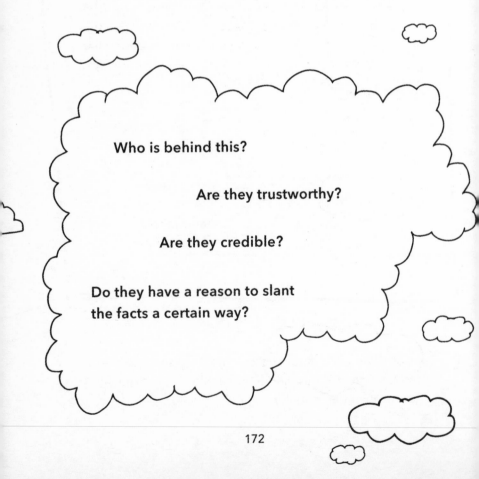

Who is behind this?

Are they trustworthy?

Are they credible?

Do they have a reason to slant the facts a certain way?

Once you've worked out the source and know their point of view, you know how much weight to give what they're saying. Sometimes, you're trying to decide on whether something presented as fact is true. In that case, use the journalistic trick of triangulation: if you can find three good, separate sources backing up the statement, it should mean it's fact and not fiction.

But sometimes what you're reading is less about a statistic or stone cold fact and more about opinion. The key to biased information like this is to seek out the opposing point of view. Then you can figure out what you believe. So if you read the *Daily Mail* now, why not read the *Guardian* too?

TOOL THREE: BREAK OUT OF YOUR COMFORT ZONE

We know that the editor of a newspaper decides which stories go on their pages or website.

But you might think that what appears on your social media feeds is random. You would be wrong. They also have an editor.

That digital editor isn't controlled by an irate newspaper owner – it's an algorithm. Imagine a comedy cartoon character who gets fatter with every piece of information or knowledge it eats. Well, every time you click 'Like', share a story or post an emoji, you are feeding your own Algo-beast. This fattened monster dictates exactly what you see and read on your timeline. It spies on your habits, likes and interests, often feeding back what it's devoured to advertisers who work out what stuff you might be tempted to buy. You might have spotted this if you've ever bought t-shirts or a pair of shoes online, and found them suddenly popping up in an ad on Facebook or Snapchat.

It's the same with news and current affairs. Social media decides which stories it shows you based on your past behaviour and what interests you on a daily basis – not in terms of global importance. Mark Zuckerberg, the founder of Facebook, justified his website's use of algorithms like this: 'A squirrel dying in front of your house may be more relevant to your interests right now than people dying in Africa.'

But there's one big problem with showing people what they already know or have shown a previous interest in: it doesn't push their boundaries. It doesn't make you learn about what you don't know or help you see things from other people's perspective. With every click, Facebook decides if you're conservative or liberal and shows you stories that reinforce your beliefs. Google uses similar algorithms to tailor your searches. Results can depend on which computer you're using and where you live. To test this, try asking a friend who lives in another country to search for the same thing as you, then send a screenshot of your results to each other – see how different they are.

The long and the short of all this is that you need to break out of this comfort zone. You don't want to only be shown points of view that are the same as your own. It's nice to believe that everyone thinks like you do – newspapers rely on their readers wanting stories that agree with the papers' own political viewpoint – but if you're to get a more rounded, truthful view of events then you need to slay the Algo-beast and broaden your horizons.

You can do this by seeking out opposing points of view, reading what they are saying and understanding how they justify their opinion – it might just make you change your mind. Even if it doesn't, you need to know how the other side thinks if you're going to take a stand.

177

TOOL FOUR : DETECT FAKE NEWS

There's a new frontline in the battle for facts and unfortunately we're right in the thick of it.

Cyberwarfare

In December 2016, the spy chief of MI6, codenamed 'C', gave a speech in a posh wood-panelled conference room deep in the Secret Intelligence Service headquarters. He revealed a serious threat to the UK from propaganda and cyber attacks. C, also known as Alex Younger, described how war was being waged by foreign countries using the web to attack democracies. He said, 'Data and the internet have turned our business on its head'.

C was talking predominantly about Russia. The European Parliament's Committee on Foreign Affairs passed a resolution in 2016 about the threat of fake news coming out of Russia. It stated that the Russian government was using fake news agencies and internet trolls to put out propaganda and weaken confidence in democratic values. The Swedes spotted it first, issuing a report that Russia was using fake news to promote splits in society. But it was the US intelligence service's revelation that Russia attempted to spread fake news during the 2016 presidential election campaign that really put the Soviet cat among the Western pigeons.

Russia has a very sophisticated propaganda machine with thousands of botnets, trolls and websites used to promote right-wing views across the internet. Using this arsenal of weapons, the fakers created and shared articles about Democrat candidate Hillary Clinton that were complete rubbish. The stories included Clinton's 'potentially fatal' health problems and her 'shady deals' with global financiers. Nobody has proved that this Russian influence swung the election result in Donald Trump's favour, but it certainly didn't help the Democrat.

The website War on the Rocks, which reports on US intelligence, also discovered a three-pronged strategy to help President Putin and his buddy, Syrian President Bashar al-Assad, gain ground in the publicity war about Syria. The three sneaks in this strategy were trolls, honeypots and hackers:

HORDE OF TROLLS

When an expert in the West criticized Syrian President Bashar al-Assad (Russia's ally), an army of trolls attacked the expert on Twitter and Facebook.

HONEYPOTS

Dozens of fake accounts pretended to be attractive young women eager to talk politics with Americans and catch them out, especially those working in the national security sector.

HACKERS

The Syrian Electronic Army's hacker operation waited until Twitter users clicked on dubious links sent out by the trolls and honeypots, then set out to hack those accounts.

War on the Rocks says this is just the beginning. They believe that Russia and its other intelligence-savvy ally, Iran, are still hard at work trying to disrupt all public confidence in democracies. All of which means there's a lot of news trash floating around the internet, masquerading as responsible reporting. But to be credible, activists must make sure that they're promoting and repeating information from solid sources.

That means you need to be vigilant to see through the fake, absolutely-not-true, definitely-planted-to-trick-you stories.

Spotting the fake news

Here are some pointers that often give the game away:

SPOTTING FAKE NEWS

- A SENSATIONAL CLAIM IN THE HEADLINE THAT ISN'T PROVED IN THE STORY
- NO AUTHOR NAME
- THE WEBSITE DOESN'T HAVE AN 'ABOUT' PAGE THAT MAKES IT CLEAR WHO'S BEHIND IT
- THE WEBSITE DOESN'T HAVE A .CO.UK OR .COM ADDRESS
- THERE ARE NO HYPERLINKS IN THE STORY TO BACK UP THE 'FACTS'
- A GOOGLE SEARCH DOESN'T FIND ANY SIMILAR STORIES
- THE SITE LOOKS SIMILAR TO A REAL NEWS ONE, BUT ALSO LOOKS A BIT ODD
- A GOOGLE SEARCH FOR THE IMAGE REVEALS IT WAS USED FOR A DIFFERENT STORY OR TAKEN IN ANOTHER YEAR

When you get fooled

If you find out later that you have circulated something fake, do the right thing. We are all responsible for keeping our social reach as honest as possible – so delete the original post and tell those you shared it with that it was bullshit. If we all get used to correcting our fake facts, we can keep our feeds truthful ... or as truthful as possible with a bunch of nefarious people trying to catch us out.

In November 2016, Buzzfeed reported that teenagers in Macedonia had launched at least 140 US politics websites with names like WorldPoliticus.com and DonaldTrumpNews.co to promote fake stories in the run-up to the presidential election. The websites said their sources were unnamed FBI agents in stories that claimed Hillary Clinton would be indicted for crimes related to an email scandal. The Macedonian teenagers didn't care about Trump winning the Presidential election; they cared about the money they could make from clicks on their Facebook pages. They worked out that false, sensational stories got the most clicks when appealing to Trump supporters. And it's not just politics websites. One 16-year-old said he also runs a health site that averages 1 million views a month.

Tackling the fakery

Facebook has become the main source of news for 18–24-year-olds, so its influence is huge. But both Facebook and Google have been criticised for not doing enough to weed out fake news. In late 2016, Facebook added a fact-check label to dubious stories, grouping them together and disputing their content. Facebook founder Mark Zuckerberg said he would rather flag up inaccurate articles than ban them.

> **II** *In a free society, it's important that people have the power to share their opinion, even if others think they're wrong.* **II**

But Zuckerberg flipped this opinion in the run-up to the 2017 general election. Facebook ramped up its fake news offensive, deleting tens of thousands of bogus profiles and refusing to promote posts that looked implausible.

The social media giant also supported Full Fact – a fact checking charity – and joined up with newsrooms to try to spot misinformation during the election campaign.

Using algorithms, it cracked down on dodgy info – identifying articles that people read but didn't like or share, suspecting that the reader was unconvinced by its truthfulness. It's not an exact science but at least they're trying to start weeding out the bullshit.

EDITING A STUDENT NEWSPAPER

Jennifer Sterne kicked off her activism career aged 10, masterminding a school strike over a new rule that shortened playtime breaks. She planned a playground occupation; everyone refused to go back to class until break times were restored. It worked. She went on to become the editor of Manchester University's *Mancunion* student newspaper.

'One of the biggest challenges for us nowadays is spotting fake news. It wasn't really a thing when I first started. I just read stuff on Facebook and thought, "If it's on Facebook and looks like a news site then it's news, of course it is". But now I'm checking every single thing on Facebook. I'm clicking on it and thinking, "Is that real? Is that true?" I'm probably lucky because I was inside the [journalism] bubble when fake news became an issue, so I'm more aware of what is fake and what isn't. I think it's made [the staff of the *Mancunion*] more likely to check things, triple-check things; we're not just accepting stuff, so that leads to better stories.'

187

TOOL FIVE :
TRACK
BREAKING NEWS

Whatever you are keen to make some noise about, you will need to keep up to speed with the very latest developments.

You can't rock up to a confrontation with the decision-makers or address a meeting of potential supporters and expect to be taken seriously if you're not properly briefed. It only takes one smart arse to reel off some fresh statistics or quote from a recent report that you haven't read to deflate your argument. So you'll need to turn bloodhound to track down the very latest info.

Not so long ago, people could only get news at just a few allotted times during the day. It may sound quaint, but they would tune into the radio or TV set when the news was 'on'. If you missed a bulletin, you'd just have to wait for the next one a few hours later. Alternatively you could wait until the paper dropped on to the doormat the next morning with yesterday's news.

Then 24-hour news came along. Sky News and CNN told us that we should be able to tune in whenever we felt like it to find out what was going on. Sometimes this has led to a merry-go-round of stories on repeat, with anchormen and women telling us about constant non-existent 'developments'. But where 24-hour news comes into its own is with breaking news. On 11 September 2001, 24-hour news meant that a worldwide audience of millions watched as planes were used as weapons to attack the World Trade Center and other targets.

The introduction of social media has taken breaking news to a whole new level. It has turned everyone with a smartphone into eyes on the ground and their own news editor. You get to choose which stories to follow and from which source.

Some stories that broke first on social media are:

When you're trying to follow a breaking story, it can be a bit bewildering – there are billions of tweets, blogs, Snapchats and Periscope feeds all competing for your click, and it can be difficult to spot which content is relevant and trustworthy.

Keep in mind the following things when deciding whether a breaking story should be taken seriously:

→ News that breaks first on social media often hasn't been verified by professional journalists unless it's from a recognisable news outlet – so take it with a pinch of salt

→ Stories can spread across countries and continents like lightning, so make sure that you know where the story originated

→ Breaking news can be posted by anyone claiming to have spoken to 'official sources' – it doesn't mean that they have

→ Comments are often added by people with little knowledge but lots of opinions, so check your facts

Twittering

Let's start with that mother of all news-alerters: Twitter. Many of us rely on the little blue bird to tell us if news is breaking. According to a poll in 2016, Twitter users get their news from the platform in three main ways:

from scrolling their timeline

from clicking on trending topics

30%

from specific searches

If you've never used a Twitter dashboard app before, such as Tweetdeck, you're about to become a Twitter super-user. It's a great way to get rid of the spammers who use hashtags to jump into breaking news searches and post fake stories. The deck can be organised into columns to help you focus on certain users or hashtags, and it also lets you block unwanted rubbish.

There are a few giveaways to look out for when spotting a spammer:

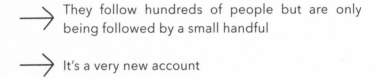 They follow hundreds of people but are only being followed by a small handful

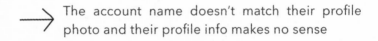 It's a very new account

The account name doesn't match their profile photo and their profile info makes no sense

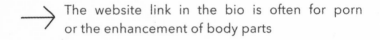 The website link in the bio is often for porn or the enhancement of body parts

It's easy to get rid of useless spammers like these – just click the arrow to the left of the tweet and hit the block line. You can also limit which users' tweets you see by selecting those who are actually close to an incident. Imagine a bomb has gone off in Bradford; if you put into the search 'near:Bradford within:threekilometres', it will only give you tweets from people within a 3-km radius of the city. Anyone pretending to be posting pictures of the incident from Brazil or the Balkans won't get a look-in.

When searching for eyewitness accounts of an event, it's good to think about how they will be thinking – to help you predict what they might tweet. Imagine the language they would use, including swear words or acronyms like WTF.

Aggregate news websites

We don't only have Twitter or Facebook to monitor current events – there are websites set up specifically to track them. Newsnow.co.uk is one of a few breaking news sites that list the content of news websites, newspapers and blogs. All the links are in one place, and it separates the stories by when they were posted, so you know which is most up to date. It also splits the stories into geographical and topical categories.

Go vintage

Many of the traditional press outlets, such as newspapers and TV channels, will track a breaking story or live event with minute-by-minute live blogs. This can be a useful way of understanding the timeline of events and the reactions of key people – handy to know when you're trying to identify which VIPs might support your campaign.

Live streams

Live-streaming tools such as Periscope and Facebook Live are great if there's someone actually at an event or incident you want to follow. However, remember that you're getting one person's viewpoint – they're not likely to be a journalist who's been trained to look for both sides of a story. That personal viewpoint can be a good thing, of course, just so long as you understand its limitations.

There's always a risk when watching live events unfold that something upsetting or disturbing might come up. Facebook Live has come unstuck with several deaths being broadcast on its site. Traditional news outlets have strict rules as to what they will show and what is censored; while live websites try to stop disturbing material from being shown, they don't always succeed.

Snapchat

Snapchat has a daily audience of 166 million users, with 45 per cent of them aged 18–24. It's a great way to follow campaigns or protests. One useful tool is its Geofilter, which allows you to search in a particular location. Just plug in the co-ordinates of a protest to see what people on the ground have shared.

At demonstrations on college campuses during President Trump's inauguration, citizen journalists used the platform to talk live into the camera about the protests and beamed live pictures of unrest and subsequent violence. It wasn't balanced reporting, but it was very different from the live broadcasts coming out of the established media.

197

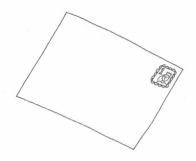

TOOL SIX :
GET YOUR MESSAGE OUT

Talking about how you want to change the world is one thing. But if you're going to actually do it, you need to stop talking about it and start really taking action.

That begins with writing out exactly what it is you stand for and what you want to change on this planet. Once you've done that, your campaign will have started.

199

Blogging

If you feel that what you have to say is unique, you should probably start blogging. Chances are that if something is inspiring you to shout about it, it will probably have the same effect on others. Get a blog out there, push it all over social media and you'll have created a channel to communicate through.

REMEMBER, WHEN BLOGGING:

* KEEP IT TIGHT AND TO THE POINT — SHORTER POSTS ARE QUICK TO CATCH ATTENTION
* THINK ABOUT WHO IT'S AIMED AT — CONSIDER WHAT WILL INTEREST YOUR READERS
* EXPRESS YOUR OWN OPINION — THERE'S NO POINT SITTING ON THE FENCE WITH YOUR WRITING
* BACK UP YOUR CLAIMS WITH FACTS, LINKING TO RESEARCH AND KEY INFORMATION
* KEEP IT CHATTY, NO ONE WANTS TO PLOUGH THROUGH HEAVY LANGUAGE
* RE-READ IT BEFORE POSTING — DO SPELL AND GRAMMAR CHECKS BECAUSE YOU'LL BE TAKEN LESS SERIOUSLY IF THERE ARE TYPOS.

Vlogging

You might prefer to just put yourself in front of a camera and become a vlogger. Get your vlogs right and you could even make some money down the line.

→ A smartphone is all you really need. You can splurge some cash on a full HD DSLR camera if you really want, but if you're just getting going, pulling out your phone will do just fine

→ Think about the audio – make sure your viewers can hear what you're saying. If you're using a phone, it's a good idea to use a second phone sitting closer to your face to record the sound. You just need to sync the sound with the video when you edit. If you're using a proper camera, they usually have a built-in microphone. Some even have a mic jack for separate wired microphones, which is even better

→ Edit your video – cut away the mistakes or the babble to keep your viewers hanging on for longer. Windows Movie Maker or iMovie are pre-installed on most computers, so if you've got one, you've got an edit suite

→ Distribute it online – set up a YouTube account and be creative with your username so that you're memorable

→ Get on social media – push your vlogs on Snapchat, Twitter and Facebook to maximize your hits. A little self-promotion goes a long way

→ Piggyback for success – you can increase your number of views by posting a vlog in response to a well- known vlogger. You'll get a knock-on effect without trying too hard

→ Start making money – once you're getting a reputation in the vlogging community, you could strive to become a YouTube partner. You'll need a few thousand hits first, but once you're there, YouTube will give you money to include ads on your videos. Cash to spend on your campaign!

Going mainstream

Getting the attention of the mainstream media might seem tricky, but you can do it if you understand how it operates. Planning editors focus on stories that have a peg. This is a key day that relates to something like an event or an anniversary providing a reason to report on something. For instance, if you're launching an environmental campaign you could peg it to 5 June: World Environment Day. Or if you want to protest about human rights abuses in Egypt, hold it on the day the Egyptian president visits the UK, or when Amnesty International or Human Rights Watch publish a new report on the subject.

Remember, planning editors get hundreds of press releases and emails vying for their attention each day. You need to make sure that your campaign stands out! The national papers will be more interested in your cause if you get the backing of a famous face; the local papers will probably turn up if your local MP is on board. Much like social media, if you can demonstrate you have a large number of supporters then you'll get more coverage in mainstream media. Turning click-activism into people turning up to show support is the key.

TOOL SEVEN : CREATE YOUR STORY

It's all very well putting your message out there, but you have to grab the attention of others to join you as well.

And with so much stuff competing for our attention, how do you punch through the videos of badly behaved pandas to get your campaign talked about?

205

Ever watched one of the TV talent shows and wondered why the audience picked one act over another when you thought the loser was the better singer? It could be that the story behind the act caught people's imagination.

THE AUTISTIC GUY

who summoned up the courage
to stand on the stage.

THE BUSKERS

who earned pennies standing in the cold
before this chance at a big break.

THE HEARTBROKEN GIRL

who wrote about being dumped, making
the TV show her revenge.

We are suckers for stories that we can relate to. And when we empathise with those involved, we're far more likely to take action.

ALAN KURDI SHAMES THE WORLD

By September 2015, the Syrian conflict had been raging for four-and-a-half years. The fighting arrived at the northern town of Kobani and one couple, Abdullah and Rehanna, decided they had to escape. They had relatives in Canada but had been told it was almost impossible to get asylum there. Even so, the couple decided to get out. They packed up what they could carry and set off with their two sons, five-year-old Ghalib and three-year-old Alan, to cross the border into Turkey.

Once there they made it to the coast, where they paid some people-traffickers for places on a boat going from the coastal town of Bodrum to the Greek island of Kos. But the boat wasn't seaworthy and it sank during the passage; only Abdullah survived. Alan's little body washed up on a Turkish beach days later, and a photojournalist took a picture.

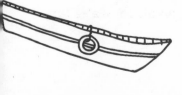

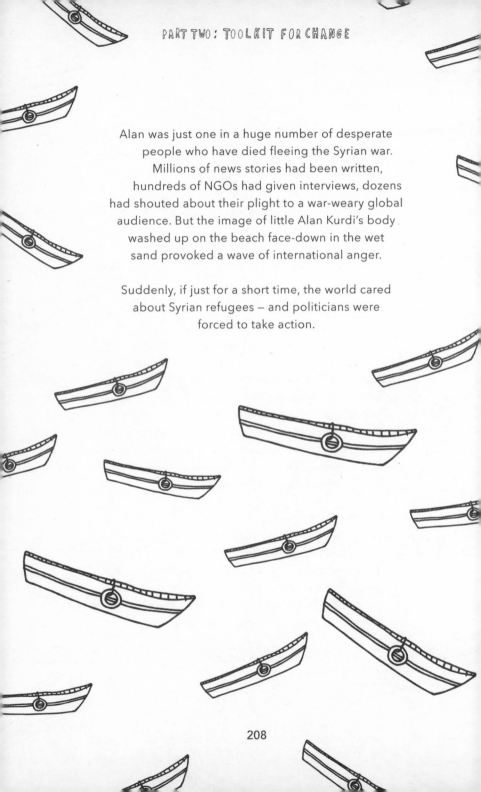

Alan was just one in a huge number of desperate people who have died fleeing the Syrian war. Millions of news stories had been written, hundreds of NGOs had given interviews, dozens had shouted about their plight to a war-weary global audience. But the image of little Alan Kurdi's body washed up on the beach face-down in the wet sand provoked a wave of international anger.

Suddenly, if just for a short time, the world cared about Syrian refugees – and politicians were forced to take action.

If the issue you care about is local, it can be more difficult to make other people care. If the campaign doesn't lend itself to empathy, the personalities involved might be interesting enough to create a hook.

If not, you might have to rely on an awesome slogan!

TOOL EIGHT: CONQUER SOCIAL MEDIA

Getting the word out about a campaign or protest used to be so much tougher, involving letters, telephones, leaflets and door-knocking.

Thankfully it's much easier today. Social media can get your call to arms whizzing through the world's fibre-optics at hypersonic speed.

It's particularly great for reaching out to young people. One opinion poll found that 34 per cent of 18–24-year-olds were politically influenced by social media, compared to just 13 per cent of the population in general.

> Qamar Ayoubi is 19. She fled the fighting in Damascus, Syria in 2013. Now she attends a sixth form in Reading. Qamar has become an activist so she can help people understand what's happening in her home country.

"

I think it's generally known that the Arab Spring came about through the use of social media. You couldn't really say a lot out on the streets or face-to-face, but you were sort of protected behind a screen. You could get your voice across.

I feel like [social media] lets you be much more organised as well. And once something's been said, it's been said – the debate is out there. Whereas if people are having a discussion between themselves, the chances of other people seeing it and getting to know their thoughts are [smaller]. Our generation is aware of the potential. **"**

Social media can also introduce you to like-minded people, as well as helping you stay connected with fellow protesters once your action gets going. Here are nine need-to-know social media resources for any serious campaigner.

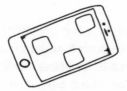

Facebook

If you're just starting out with online activism, Facebook gives you the chance to test the water. You can put something out there and see how much of a reaction you get. The chances are that if you are angry about something, others are feeling the same way. Once you've caused a stir, you can ask who's up for doing something about it. That's what happened in Egypt:

In June 2010, Egyptian Wael Ghonim was browsing his Facebook page while abroad in the UAE when he came across the photo of a 28-year-old guy from Alexandria who had been killed by police. Wael decided to reach out on Facebook for a reaction. He created the Facebook page 'We are all Khaled Said', and in just three days, 100,000 Egyptians had joined his page. It started a conversation where followers would crowdsource ideas and share news of other stories of abuse. It became the most followed page in the Arab world, attracting more people then traditional news organisations and famous celebrity sites. By January 2011, after a revolution in nearby Tunisia and with 300,000 followers now on the

page, Wael decided to call for action. He posted an event named 'A Revolution against Corruption, Injustice and Dictatorship'. In just a few days the invitation reached over 1 million people and 100,000 confirmed they would turn up. On 25 January, Egyptians flooded the streets and called for change.

Facebook's reach is bigger than Twitter's when used as a campaign tool, but it has some limitations that can restrict your actions.

→ A real name is required to open a page, so you need to put your identity to the campaign. (Not always a plus for some revolutionaries!)

→ Facebook's algorithms can impact the growth of a campaign (the Algo-beast strikes again!)

→ Getting on to news feeds sometimes means paying to be promoted.

However, it is a good platform to communicate with those who have already pledged allegiance to your cause. Publicising an event is quick and easy from your FB page.

Twitter

Get your 140 characters right and the little blue bird can be your campaign's best friend. Once you start to stir some attention, you might only need a hashtag to get people moving – but at first, use your tweet as a way of directing people to a more detailed breakdown of your plan of action, such as a blog, vlog, Facebook event or website.

THE TWITTER REVOLUTION

In 2009, Moldova held a general election that saw the Communist Party returned to power. But in a café in the capital, Chisinau, a group of friends were convinced the election results had been rigged.

25-year-old Natalia Morar and her mates wanted to protest against the election fraud and decided to stage a flash mob. They put the word out via Twitter, blogs, texts and websites. Only a few hours later, 15,000 people came out on to the streets. They had captured the frustration of the people, especially younger ones, in one of Europe's poorest countries. When the protests grew in number, they were hijacked by a violent faction that fought the police and broke into the parliament buildings. The authorities soon stopped the demonstrations and a crackdown against all dissent followed.

But the decision-makers had been put on notice. Greater transparency was demanded and eventually agreed upon.

Twitter can also be a powerful platform for challenging the bias and spin put out by politicians and the media. Social media naturally tends to rebuff attempts at political control.

On Remembrance Sunday in 2015, the spin turned against Labour leader Jeremy Corbyn. He was accused of disrespecting the wreath-laying ceremony at London's Cenotaph by not bowing enough. The story got traction on Twitter until photographs were posted of Corbyn going above and beyond. He had stayed behind after the ceremony, when all the other VIPs had gone to a champagne reception, to talk to veterans and shake their hands. Social media managed to spin the spin in the opposite direction.

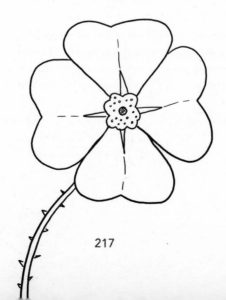

217

Messaging apps

You can just use WhatsApp for gossip and chat, but it can do so much more. By putting groups of people into one conversation you can share the word about your campaign far from prying eyes. It can be used to publicise an event or pass on information. If you don't have WhatsApp, you can use similar services with Blackberry, Viber or Facebook Messenger.

Messaging apps have also been used to great effect by more traditional political parties.

INDIAN ELECTIONS OF 2014

WhatsApp was a good barometer of how the election was going among its 40 million users in India. The little green speech bubble was used to gather political preferences, conduct polling and organise campaign volunteers. The tech-savvy political parties sent out campaign info to their volunteers, who in turn created a waterfall through their chain of contacts. But WhatsApp isn't always a positive for those on the campaign trail. It backfired when India's prime ministerial candidate, Narendra Modi, who had stood as a single man, was outed on WhatsApp as married. Not the crime of the century you might think, but he had risen through the ranks of a grassroots Hindu nationalist organisation where celibacy is expected. Oops!

Reddit

Reddit is a great source for up-to-the-minute movements, comment and links to people who are like-minded. Its subreddits mean that you can search for the issues you care about and meet other subscribers virtually.

MONITORING FERGUSON

During 2014 unrest in Ferguson, Missouri, USA, following the fatal shooting of a black man by a white police officer, Reddit set up a live feed page that was maintained 24 hours a day by 10 moderators.

The page brought together a range of sources including tweets, YouTube videos and web content as well as police scanner reports and news articles. In doing so, Reddit created not just a breaking news platform but also a source for protest plans.

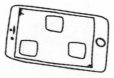

Instagram

Instagram can go beyond photo uploads to be used as a way of unifying people to a cause, or to voice mutual concerns. Eyewitness accounts, videos and images often draw activists to monitor and add content to the app. During the Ferguson unrest, 272,562 people posted using the hashtag #ferguson in one day. It's been used to tell other personal stories too.

AMBER AMOUR

27-year-old American Amber Amour launched a shocking media campaign in 2014 that took Instagram to another level. She posted pictures of herself immediately after being raped in Cape Town, South Africa, and shared what had happened. It wasn't the first time she had been attacked and it made for difficult reading, but it sparked a huge conversation on the internet.

YouTube

The right video, GIF or meme can send your protest message around the world in an instant. However, unfortunately there is no set formula that makes a video go viral. (If you manage to work it out, you are going to make millions.) Most political parties create awful 'party political broadcasts' that go out around election time and bore TV viewers to tears. However, there is one party that is trying to reflect the way people are entertained nowadays: the Green Party.

They caused a stir in 2015 when they put out a party political broadcast on YouTube that used lookalikes of the other parties' leaders singing in a boy band in unison. The message was that all the other parties were just saying the same thing. YouTube viewers loved it, but it was the Greens' next broadcast that was the real hit. This time, the other leaders were 5-year-olds playing out their politics in the nursery school playground.

Did it win them extra votes? Who knows – but it was very funny.

FireChat

This app can be used as a great protest organiser should the internet go down or if you're offline. The app uses Bluetooth or Wi-Fi in what's termed 'mesh networking', to connect users to each other. Most phones go through a centralised cellular network but a mesh network is decentralised as you're communicating locally – this means you can't be intercepted, monitored or blocked.

HONG KONG UMBRELLA MOVEMENT

Remember the 14-year-old from the introduction, who started a protest movement against Chinese propaganda? On Facebook that activist, Joshua Wong, posted that protesters should download FireChat in case the internet was cut off or the system couldn't cope with the amount of media traffic during the protest. In one week, about half a million people downloaded the app, leading to over five million chat sessions. Ilt wasn't the first time FireChat had helped a protest movement communicate – the Taiwanese Sunflower Student demonstrators had kept in touch with each other both inside and outside of the parliament building they occupied. But the Umbrella protestors took it to another level.

Meetup.com

Meetup.com has a whole section designed to help burgeoning movements get off the ground. There are some unlikely groups but it means there's something for everyone! Here are three random groups:

→ Beers with Bremainers has almost 1,200 members (if you want to meet up and talk about the UK leaving the EU all night!)

→ Lets-build-our-own-apartments-in-london group, with upwards of 140 members

→ GlobalNet21: Recreating Our Futures has over 7,600 members discussing major issues in the twenty-first century

Crowdvoice

Crowdvoice works like Storify, the site that lets you create a web page pulling in lots of different sources – but it does the same for protests.

It's a great platform for activists who want to keep up to date with facts, figures and developing stories relating to their own campaigns and protests.

The downsides of social media

Social media is a fantastic tool for spreading campaign messages around the world. But there are dangers to avoid when you whizz around the huge social media universe.

DEPENDENCY

Dependence on social media can hamper a movement or a campaign. While it might mean that you reach huge numbers of people, it won't necessarily motivate them to do anything more than just click on the share or like button. If you're looking to convert the numbers of likes or Facebook followers into people actually getting out on to the streets, social media can stall your progress.

Social media can also dilute your leadership. It doesn't take much for someone to draw followers away from your campaign and into their own. You need to be proactive once you've launched your big idea, engaging your community with more than just the Like button.

BAD BEHAVIOUR

It's easy to misbehave online. You're often anonymous apart from your username, so people find they are quicker to criticise or attack others from the safety of their laptop. It's bad enough when it's one-on-one, but when single voices join together, the result can be disastrous.

Wael Ghonim, whose Facebook page we learned about earlier, says the social media that helped bring about Egyptian president Mubarak's downfall also did huge damage to those trying to bring about a consensus afterwards. Social media helped to divide people through misinformation, rumours and hate speech.

If you're going to use social media to launch and run a campaign, you're probably going to interact with people who don't agree with you. Debate and even a solid argument is a good way to fine-tune your opinions and help you sharpen your campaign literature. But if debate turns into trolling or worse, you have three options: you can ignore the barbed comments, taking the high ground; you can take the troll on by being reasonable and exposing them as trolls; and for extreme behaviour, you can reach for the block button, or even report it to the police.

THE EMPIRE MIGHT STRIKE BACK

Don't forget: the authorities can use social media too. If they want to, unscrupulous decision-makers can spread disinformation to send protestors to the wrong location or put out fake news to frighten them away.

If you are targeting dodgy decision-makers in government, it's possible that they'll use your social media pages to gather intelligence. To mask your location when rallying your supporters, you could use a proxy server that protects your identity and location online by hiding your IP address.

Social media is a springboard

Over the centuries, activism – whether by French Revolutionaries or the Suffragettes – generally meant getting off your backside and taking to the streets. Social media has changed all that, making it easier for people to get involved than ever before.

However, as Jennifer Sterne, the former editor of the *Mancunion* student newspaper says, getting involved online often isn't enough.

"

As well as using social media to rally young people, we need to get out on the streets and start shouting. We're not being listened to and it's not OK. People are just starting to get annoyed, and to realise that if they don't shout out then people like Trump get elected. That's what happens. Unfortunately we needed that wake-up call to realise that we can't just re-tweet something and it will be OK, you have to get out and shout a little bit louder. If [other people] start hearing that you're doing it, they'll join in.

"

A demonstration or a march or a sit-in – or any other style of direct protest – invites people to actually turn up to show their support. And there is still no greater show of solidarity today than being somewhere in person.

TOOL NINE: SPEAK LOUD AND PROUD

It's one thing to know what's wrong with the world and how you want it to change.

It's another thing entirely to know how to inspire other people so they'll join your campaign. History is full of people who have changed the course of events by making an amazing speech. But speech-giving can be tough unless you've done your homework and got over the nerves. Very few of us relish the idea of speaking in front of an audience. American comedian Jerry Seinfeld summed it up like this:

❚❚ *Speaking in front of a crowd is considered the number one fear of the average person. This means, to the average person, if you have to be at a funeral, you would rather be in the casket than doing the eulogy.* **❚❚**

Preparing a speech

So let's work on the skills needed to turn you into a great orator. When you speak, whether to one person or a big group, you are sending out signals. The language you use, the stories you tell and the image you project all send out signals that have nothing to do with your actual message. So you need to get those signals right or your big idea could be muted or even lost.

Six big tips for coming across well in a speech are:

BE PASSIONATE

You have to show that you care
about your message.

USE HUMOUR

If you want to keep people listening, it might
just help to make them smile.

SAY SOMETHING UNEXPECTED

If you just repeat what the audience expects
you to say, they'll soon start to fall asleep.

TELL A STORY

The best way to engage an audience
is to draw them in with a tale they can relate to.

KEEP IT TIGHT

Stay focused on your message
and avoid rambling.

PRACTISE
PRACTISE PRACTISE PRACTISE

Of course, speaking confidently is the best tip of all. The safest way to ensure you don't get that tongue-tied, dry-mouthed, rabbit-in-the-headlights look is to work out what format your speech will take. Beware – do not learn your lines! It might be tempting to memorise your speech like an actor, but you risk drying up and having nothing in your head to say. And reeling sentences off like a parrot means you will probably deliver them without passion and your audience will switch off. It's much better to use a technique called 'babble boxes'. Babble boxes are like little parcels of facts, quotes, figures and information that help you to break down your thoughts and deliver inspiring speeches.

Let's take an example. Say you want to persuade your audience that they should cycle to school or work all summer instead of driving or taking public transport. You can use babble boxes to separate out your key ideas.

233

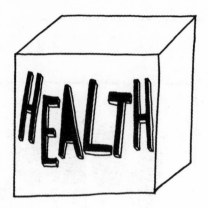

→ Makes you fitter

→ Might help you lose weight

→ Helps you drink more water

→ Doesn't use fuel

→ Without your cars, there'll be fewer traffic jams and less pollution

→ Saves fare or fuel cost

→ Gives you more time in bed because it's quicker

→ It's easier to park a bike than a car

Once you've got your thoughts down, it's time to work out your framework – how will you use this information to construct a speech? Well, you can either dip into different boxes one point at a time, or you can empty each box one by one – it's up to you.

235

It could also be up to the audience. The benefit of babble boxes is that you can adapt your speech right in the middle of saying it. If you start to talk through your list of health benefits and it looks like the audience is zoning out, you could tell a story or make them smile to get back their attention.

Once they're paying attention, you can mention some more sensible points from any of the other boxes. Keep emptying the boxes until you feel the audience has got your message, then finish on a high – maybe leave them thinking about all the bags of guilt-free crisps they could have eaten if they had only cycled to hear you.

Engaging with the audience

Now that we've got our content down, we need to think about how we look – and I'm not talking about hair, make-up or clothes. I'm referring to how we engage with the audience.

Your body language and eye contact can often send out just as many signals as the words you use.

236

Some more tips to remember are:

→ **LOOK**
directly at the audience when you speak

→ **STAND UP** straight

→ **NEVER** cross your arms

→ **RELAX** your hands

→ **DO NOT** fill the gaps
Umm, so, you know and like are all concentration killers!

Finding inspiration

It's time to get a little inspiration from some of the world's best orators (and others who just came up with some good one-liners).

"
We shall fight on the beaches, we shall fight on the landing grounds, we shall fight in the fields and in the streets, we shall fight in the hills, we shall never surrender, and if, which I do not for a moment believe, this island or a large part of it were subjugated and starving, then our Empire beyond the seas, armed and guarded by the British Fleet, would carry on the struggle, until, in God's good time, the New World, with all its power and might, steps forth to the rescue and the liberation of the old. **"**

– Sir Winston Churchill,
Prime Minister during the Second World War

238

**" *And so, my fellow Americans:
ask not what your country can do for you
– ask what you can do for your country.* "**

– John F Kennedy,
US president 1961–63

**" *In the end, we will remember not the words of
our enemies, but the silence of our friends.* "**

– Martin Luther King, Jr,
US civil rights leader

239

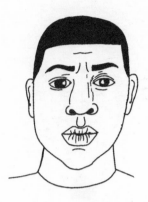

" *Rosa Parks sat so Martin Luther could walk.*
Martin Luther walked so Barack Obama could run.
Barack Obama ran so all the children could fly. **"**

– Jay-Z, US rapper

" *I don't mind if I have to sit on the floor at school.*
All I want is education. And I'm afraid of no one. **"**

– Malala Yousafzai, Pakistani activist for female education

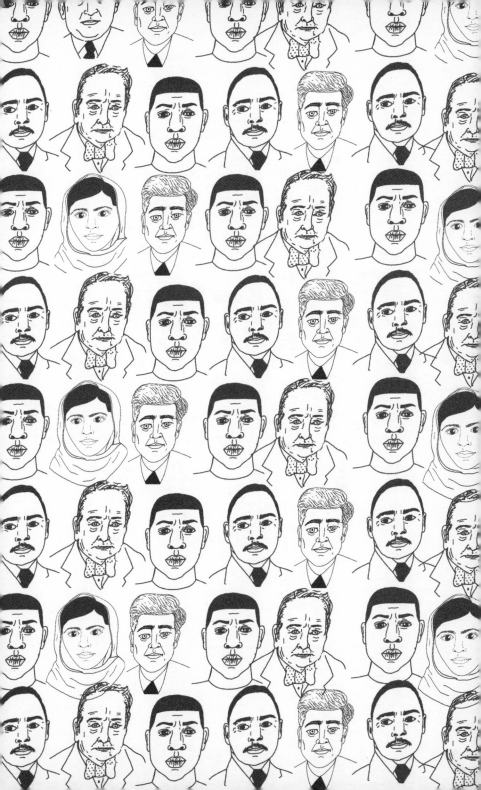

TOOL TEN: CRACK DEBATING

As well as making speeches, you will need to be able to stand up for your big idea.

That means you're going to need some verbal fencing skills to sharpen up your debating technique. Debating can seem like something that only politicians and people from posh private schools do. If you don't think you'll be having debates any time soon, remember that they don't have to be held in a fancy debating chamber – there are loads of opportunities to argue your case on social media, with friends and family, and people you meet out and about.

243

WORLD DEBATING CHAMPION COMES FROM HACKNEY

In a basement theatre just off Trafalgar Square, Ife Grillo set the room alight. This 18-year-old student from Hackney, a black guy in a blue beanie tapping ferociously on his battered iPad, was the last to speak in a debate on social media. As he argued against the proposal, his words were almost rapping, never taking his eyes off the audience, engaging through straightforward reasoning that spoke from the heart.

Ife stole the show, just like he had when he'd won the Schools' World Championship. At that competition, he'd broken the mould because all the previous winners had come from private schools.

Ife has two tips for debating success:

244

CHANNEL YOUR ANGER

1. A lot of people are angry, but don't let anyone say anger is wasteful. Channel it. Use it. For me, being angry with the world got me where I am today.

2. If you're not confident enough to speak out or debate, write a blog post. You can do that for free. There are so many ways to express your views – through music, dance, any medium, whatever works for you. But express yourself!

How to debate

MAKE A PLAN

No good military strategist goes into battle without thinking through every eventuality, and debating is the same. Plan in advance how to argue against somebody who doesn't agree with you. You could draw out the way a debate might run on a piece of paper so that you know which counter-arguments you'll need when the conversation turns. Try to sit in your opposition's shoes and work out how you would argue against yourself.

BOIL DOWN YOUR ARGUMENT

Think of your key points and work out how to explain each one in as few words as possible. If that sounds like a tall order, television news reporters are told when they start out that the story of the Second World War takes less than 2 minutes, 45 seconds to tell.

AVOID AGGRESSION

You might feel so passionately about your big idea that you can't bear to hear another point of view. Unfortunately, that's not how to win an argument. The more reasonable you sound, the more likely you'll win people around, even if it's just to a small degree.

HOARD FINGERTIP FACTS

Make sure you have done all your research and have your key facts, figures and information (babble boxes) to hand, possibly written down on a piece of paper. It's good to include your opponent's strengths and weaknesses if possible.

LISTEN TO YOUR OPPONENT

Even professional TV news anchors are sometimes accused of not listening to their interviewees. The only way to counter an argument is by carefully listening to your opponent. Don't assume that they'll come back at you with a certain position. Check that they are as opposed to your big idea as you initially thought. Then tailor your own response to that specific answer.

Taking the debate online

When even the US president is arguing on Twitter, you know you need to refine your social media debating skills. Thankfully, there are techniques you can use to help. Lady Helena Kennedy QC has made a career out of winning arguments as one of the nation's top barristers. Her handy strategy when trying to win a case is called PREP, and although it can be used offline, it's particularly helpful when taking on opponents on the internet.

PREP
=
POSITION
+
REASON
+
EXAMPLE
+
POSITION

POSITION

You need to know your own position. Work out beforehand exactly what you are trying to persuade people to accept, and make it simple. Thankfully, if it's on Twitter you've only got 140 characters to play with.

REASON

Justify your position and be reasonable. It's much harder to detect someone's tone on Twitter or Snapchat, and you can't see their facial expressions, so think twice before assuming they're being rude. Don't get personal even if provoked. If someone gets personal when arguing against you, they've lost. Just keep supporting your argument with facts and you'll win in the end.

EXAMPLE

Be ready with facts and figures to justify your stance. Never bluff, but also try not to be overwhelmed if you feel you're right but don't have the exact stats to hand.

REPEAT POSITION

To conclude, restate your point of view but don't get exasperated if you haven't won anybody over. There's no point having a protracted argument if they're not giving any ground. Your pleasant reasoning might just swing somebody round later!

Debating tricks

There are a few tricks to look out for when debating an opponent with less-than-perfect scruples.

PROVOCATION

Deliberately provoking an opponent to make them lose their temper and the audience's backing.

EXAGGERATION

Making the other side's position seem excessively unreasonable to deter the audience from that point of view – and fluster the opposition.

ALTERNATIVE FACTS

Throwing in some fake or alternative facts. This is difficult to deal with when debating in person, but you could suggest a fact-off, asking the audience to Google the 'fact'. It's easy to sort out on social media because you have Google at your fingertips.

FAKE FACTS

TOOL ELEVEN: AVOID THE HYPNOTISTS

Beware: extreme political factions are after you! Well, at least your vote.

That's one of the arguments made by the people who don't want the voting age lowered to 16 – that young, first-time voters are useful targets for those with more radical views. The theory goes that younger voters are more likely to be drawn to radical alternatives or influenced by famous faces with no political knowledge but plenty of opinion. There are two levels to this kind of persuasion: populism and radicalisation. The first is based around a charismatic leader who says he or she is everything the establishment is not. The second taps into people's disaffection with life and grooms them for extremism.

Populism

There's been a political typhoon blowing through the West and its name is populism. The word on its own is harmless enough – it means being popular to ordinary people. But in politics it has another meaning. Usually it refers to the rise of the far-right or the far-left, often accompanied by a persuasive figurehead.

'Populism' is far from a new concept – many remember it from the twentieth century when charismatic populist leaders in Latin America spoke passionately about the unhappiness of their countries' people, advocating for change. They appealed to voters by promising to spend enormous amounts of money on public services that would help the poor. This version of populism might seem positive enough, but it has been criticised for leading to huge spending costs, bad management and rampant inflation.

However, populism isn't itself aligned with either end of the political spectrum: populist leaders can come from both the far-left and the far-right. They achieve this by blaming established political parties for everything that seems to have gone wrong in their country. They win support by having a go at the ones making the decisions: the traditional rulers, the political elites.

Populist leaders split public opinion. Some see them as amazing speakers who manipulate emotions to shore up support but don't live in the real world where compromises have to be made. Others believe that they are the only ones standing up for everyday people against leaders who are incompetent and think they know best. To see how populists manage to get the support of people from opposite ends of the political spectrum, let's look at two experienced heavyweights in this arena:

HUGO CHÁVEZ

The socialist former president of Venezuela.

RECEP TAYYIP ERDOĞAN

The religiously conservative right-wing
president of Turkey.

Both these presidents claimed that they were under attack from clandestine movements in their own countries and from meddling powers abroad. They said they stood for 'real' people (as if the people who didn't back them are somehow 'unreal'). And that was how they got their power base: by scaring their people into believing that their rulers – and therefore the whole country – was under attack. However, once they had secured the necessary support, the two leaders had very different remedies to solve the problems they had diagnosed: radical socialism in Venezuela and far-right conservativism in Turkey.

So why is populism on the rise in the West at the moment?

Well, there's been a perfect storm that has allowed this typhoon to grow in size and strength:

→ A financial and economic crisis, leaving many people distrusting institutions

→ A lack of money and jobs, making people look for someone to blame

→ Immigration and a refugee crisis, leading people to fear that their country may change

While there are populist movements from both sides of the political spectrum today, the populism gathering pace most quickly is growing out of the far-right. Most Western nations have seen it build out of a combination of fear and, in response to that fear, exaggerated confidence. Some of the key messages that populists are using include:

CLASS DIVIDE

Society is divided into 'haves' and 'have-nots'.

ECONOMIC INSECURITY

Jobs and wealth will be taken by outsiders.

PATRIOTISM

We should be proud of our country.

NATIONALISM

Our country is better than the rest.

Some of the right-wing populist parties in Europe include France's National Front, led by Marine Le Pen; Hungary's Fidesz, led by Viktor Orbán; and the Netherlands' Party for Freedom, led by Geert Wilders. In the UK, UKIP has been the strongest populist presence.

However, despite all the successes that European right-wing populism has seen, there is one populist leader of the twenty-first century who eclipses them all: American president Donald Trump. Here are just some of the claims he's made:

Biggest inauguration crowd ever

Biggest election win

Voter fraud cost him the popular vote

Those protesting against him are paid professionals

Polls reflecting poorly on him are fake

Media that criticises him is the enemy of the people

Why did President Trump make these claims? Because he campaigned as the leader of 'the people', standing up to establishment elites. He won the election, so that must mean that all of the people support him – and any poll or newspaper that says differently is lying.

This is why populist leaders are dangerous: they claim to be on the side of 'the people', but they don't accept the rights or opinions of anyone who doesn't support them. Populist parties threaten the very nature of democracy. However, there's an even more sinister group out there, trying to persuade us round to their twisted point of view: extremists who try to radicalise us.

Radicalisation

If you're unhappy about something and there's no way for you to channel that discontent – if you feel you cannot express it, or protest about it – then you could be drawn in by people who want to exploit that voicelessness.

They might lead you down a dark, desperate hole of hate and horror that ends with terrorism. Here are two charismatic leaders who made it their life's work to radicalise people:

ADOLF HITLER

Hitler was an exceptional orator. His charisma stirred millions of frustrated Germans to follow him into a war by telling them what they wanted to hear: that they were the greatest race on Earth. He commanded enormous loyalty by making his extremism sound like a democratic victory.

II All great movements are popular movements.
They are the volcanic eruptions of human passions

and emotions, stirred into activity by the ruthless Goddess of Distress or by the torch of the spoken word cast into the midst of the people. ▮▮

Hitler's extremism led to the deaths of 6 million Jews during the Holocaust.

ANJEM CHOUDARY

Anjem Choudary started life as the son of a market trader and then studied at Southampton University to become a lawyer. But in the mid-1980s, he founded a hardline network that glorified terrorism. Publically, he often stated that Britain shouldn't be a target of violent jihad because it allowed Muslim immigrants to move there. But he was actually grooming as many as 500 people to become terrorists. He posted a huge amount of propaganda online that radicalised people, as well as making public statements of extremist views.

Among his inflammatory stances were a call for Buckingham Palace to become a mosque and a refusal to condemn the 7/7 bombings in London. In 2016, he was jailed for five-and-a-half years.

You might think that the odds of radicalisation happening to you are pretty low. So let's not beat about the bush here – how do you know if you're at risk of being radicalised?

Are you having an identity or personal crisis?

Are your cries of injustice being ignored?

Do you yearn for adventure and excitement?

Do you feel your faith or culture is under threat?

Do you feel isolated?

Have you broken rules or the law before?

Do you long to belong to a community of people who think as you do?

If you think someone you know is being radicalised, the first thing to do is talk to them. Try to get them to explain their behaviour and why they might be interested in a radical group or quoting extreme ideology. Listen to their reasoning and if you think radicalisation is happening, you need to tell either a teacher if they're at school or the police. They will bring in an agency called Channel that specialises in cases of radicalisation. As well as tracking down the reasons someone is being drawn to extremism,

Channel can help with re-education, assessing health issues and housing problems, as well as providing mentoring support.

Some people argue that the way the media and the government talk about some sections of our community makes things worse. A report by retired judge Baroness Butler-Sloss found widespread unhappiness with how the media reported on religion, particularly Islam. Her research found that the press referred to extreme forms of Islam and Muslim extremists 21 times more frequently than ordinary Muslims. Demonising one section of the community in this way increases the chances of young people becoming disaffected and isolated. And this leaves them even more vulnerable to being radicalised.

In the battle against extremism, governments have granted the police and other security services sweeping powers to monitor attempts of radicalisation. But there's a danger here: that the state might try to intimidate peaceful protesters with those powers.

In 2016, it emerged that a secretive police unit had been monitoring leading members of the Green Party. Documents revealed that an intelligence unit was spying on the Greens to discover their attitude to government cuts, police violence and the upcoming visit of the Pope. Green MP Caroline Lucas had been logged for giving a speech at an economic protest in London and attending another demonstration against the far-right in Brighton.

The above is an example of how democracy can be threatened when the state gets too powerful. Becoming politically active is a fantastic way of holding politicians to account. But BEWARE extremists telling you what you want to hear. Activism is the clever way to channel anger and frustration over something you feel strongly about. You have the power to create a buzz about injustice, inequality or unfairness and to harness that energy. If you get it right you can make a huge difference, turning your fury into a fight for good.

BEWARE
BEWARE
BEWARE
BEWARE
BEWARE
BEWARE
BEWARE

TOOL TWELVE: EMBRACE YOUR SPECIALIST KNOWLEDGE

The small armies of people who conduct opinion polls are in broad agreement: if the voting age had been lowered to 16 for the 2016 EU referendum, the outcome would have been different.

Unfortunately, under-18s didn't get a say. And that's tricky, because the perspective of a young person really matters when we're debating how the country will be ruled long after today's politicians collect their pensions.

So what are the issues that matter to you? And how can your specialist knowledge – your young person's perspective – make a difference?

This isn't about being populist – I'm not trying to say that all young people have the same opinions. Instead, think of issues as dishes at an all-you-can-eat buffet. Some you will find abhorrent (Brussels sprouts?) and leave well alone. Some you will grab as essential (chips?) and prioritise on your tray. But there's room for a few more, too – so look around for dishes that you might have overlooked initially. Much like a huge spread of food, political choice is about handpicking a selection of key topics that you care about. They might lead you towards a particular political party – but they might not. The decision over how important each of these topics are is down to you. There are a whole host of issues that are specific to young people but most MPs do little about because they don't yet rely on your vote to get elected. So if you don't see a candidate worth voting for, you need to make your voice heard. The more young people vote, and the louder they speak up about issues they want to change, the more MPs will alter their policies to appeal to them.

Let's have a look at some key policy areas where young people have a unique perspective – and might have more riding on the outcome – compared to older voters.

Education

According to the pollsters, the hottest political topic for young people is the cost of further education. And with good reason: from autumn 2017, English universities are charging up to £9,250 per year. That's on top of just the average cost of living in the UK, which stands at about £12,000 per year. That makes a grand total of nearly £22,000 that a young person will have to find if they want to study for a year.

The story differs depending on where in the country you come from: it's even worse if you're studying in uber-expensive London, Welsh fees are about the same as England's, Northern Ireland students get their tuition for a lot less (£3,925) and fees for students from Scotland don't even exist. But moving to Scotland won't help someone from England get lectures for free – it's where you come from that matters. Whether you can afford education becomes a postcode lottery.

Further education used to be free – in the 1980s and early 1990s, the government even gave students grants. But in 1998, the Labour government introduced tuition fees of up to £1,000 depending on what a student's family could afford. In opposition, the Conservatives called this 'a tax on learning' and vowed to abolish the fees. But in 2006, Tory David Cameron described them as unavoidable, saying, 'The money's got to come from somewhere' – and once he was prime minister in 2010, he upped the fees.

Mental health for young people

This topic leaves teachers, parents and MPs gasping for breath. From anorexia and bulimia to cutting and even suicide, most people over the age of 25 struggle to understand the pressures that young people are under. Thinking about the factors that might improve mental health for young people is really complicated – but you're likely to understand it much more than older people.

Cost of exercise

With obesity and diabetes at epidemic levels among young people, you would think the government would be giving sports and exercise away for free. Surely the knock-on effects in the reduction of NHS costs would justify a free tennis court or swimming pool pass?

Cost and quality of housing

For most young people it feels like there's virtually no chance of getting on the property ladder this century. Which means you're looking at rented accommodation or staying with the parents for decades. Is anybody in government really concerned with the cost and quality of housing available when you're at the bottom of the pile?

The future of our planet

Our transport habits have changed hugely in the last century; a hundred years ago we travelled by steam train, electric tram or horseback because only the wealthy could afford a car. The explosion in car ownership and air travel, plus global energy demands, have transformed the demands on the world's resources.

271

Now imagine the changes likely over the next 100 years. Somehow this planet is going to have to cough up even more resources to meet those demands, but the energy sources we've been relying on most are running out. Scientists are desperately trying to get the attention of decision-makers, spelling out the terrible dangers of climate change.

This is more a problem for you than it is for today's politicians sitting in parliament, the EU, the UN and everywhere else. Their priorities are to their generation, their electorate or those that put them into power – not a potentially dystopian future that they probably won't live long enough to experience.

The younger you are, the bigger your incentive to protect this planet and take those who abuse it to task.

PROTECT
PROTECT
PROTECT
PROTECT
PROTECT
PROTECT

JOSHUA WONG'S UMBRELLA MOVEMENT

What could a 14-year-old dyslexic kid achieve when going up against the world's largest authoritarian regime? You might think not very much – but you'd be wrong. Joshua Wong realised that education in Hong Kong was to become what he calls 'Chinese brainwashing', after the government agreed to introduce China's version of history rather than an international view. Joshua didn't leave it to someone else to protest against it – he felt it was up to him and his generation to stop it happening. He set up a protest group called Scholarism and by 2012, 120,000 people joined him on a political rally.

Two years later, their protest group had grown into something much bigger – it had become a movement that went to the very heart of Hong Kong-Chinese relations. When China took over control of Hong Kong from the British in 1997, the Chinese had promised to allow free elections in 2017. But that wasn't happening – instead, China was imposing presidential candidates that it could control. Wong's group, now under the name of the Umbrella Movement, set up an unofficial referendum on the topic and the vast majority of people voted for free elections.

TIME magazine named Joshua Wong one of the most influential teens of 2014. In 2015, *Fortune* magazine named him as one of the world's greatest leaders. In 2016, aged 19, he co-founded Demosistō, a pro-democracy political party in Hong Kong.

" [2017] is the twentieth anniversary of the Hong Kong handover. I believe that before the handover no one expected a high school student could lead a demonstration of 100,000 people to join it. What I believe is that even when we're still in school and haven't graduated from college or university, we're still the ones that have to fight for the future of our city and make change in society.

After Brexit, people in the UK felt strongly about political uncertainty and stability. The younger generation can be inspired and you should know that with your courage and passion, activism on the streets can really make change to society. If you're the one that cares about democracy and human rights and freedom, it's time to join a strike and help to fight for social justice. **"**

275

THE UNIONS? PROVIDE TEMPLATES FOR THE LETTER MAKE YOUR GOAL CLE

ENT SHARE YOUR CAMPAIGN ON SOCIAL MEDIA NOMINATION FORM THE LEGIS

< YOUR HANDS DO NOT FILL THE GAPS WORLD DEBATING CHAMPION COMES FROM

IS WHO IS BEHIND THIS? INDIAN ELECTIONS OF 2014 TO SLANT THE FA

EN? PROVOCATION EXAGGERATION MONITORING FERGUSON DO THEY HAVE A R

FROM WITHIN ALTERNATIVE FACTS ARE THEY TRUSWORTHY? EDITING

ISE IN THE WEST AT THE MOMENT? ARE THEY CREDIBLE? GET YOUR MESSAG

OCIAL MEDIA SPEAK LOUD AND PROUD AVOID THE HYPNOTISTS CRACK DEBAT

THE UNIONS? PROVIDE TEMPLATES FOR THE LETTER MAKE YOUR GOAL CLE

ENT SHARE YOUR CAMPAIGN ON SOCIAL MEDIA NOMINATION FORM THE LEGIS

< YOUR HANDS DO NOT FILL THE GAPS WORLD DEBATING CHAMPION COMES FROM

I FOR QUESTIONS WHO IS BEHIND THIS? INDIAN ELECTIONS OF 2014 TO S

E SYSTEM BROKEN? PROVOCATION EXAGGERATION MONITORING FERGUSON DO TH

INDS WORKING FROM WITHIN ALTERNATIVE FACTS ARE THEY TRUSWORTH

LISM ON THE RISE IN THE WEST AT THE MOMENT? ARE THEY CREDIBLE? GET

RY CONQUER SOCIAL MEDIA SPEAK LOUD AND PROUD AVOID THE HYPNOTISTS

S PEOPLE OFF THE UNIONS? PROVIDE TEMPLATES FOR THE LETTER MAKE

ELECTION AGENT SHARE YOUR CAMPAIGN ON SOCIAL MEDIA NOMINATION FO

UR ARM RELAX YOUR HANDS DO NOT FILL THE GAPS WORLD DEBATING CHAMPIO

BEHIND THIS? INDIAN ELECTIONS OF 2014 TO SLANT THE FACTS A CERT

ATION EXAGGERATION MONITORING FERGUSON DO THEY HAVE A REASON ALAN

IN ALTERNATIVE FACTS ARE THEY TRUSWORTHY? EDITING A STUDENT

EST AT THE MOMENT? ARE THEY CREDIBLE? GET YOUR MESSAGE OUT CREAT

SPEAK LOUD AND PROUD AVOID THE HYPNOTISTS CRACK DEBATING EMBRACI

? PROVIDE TEMPLATES FOR THE LETTER MAKE YOUR GOAL CLEAR THE EXE

YOUR CAMPAIGN ON SOCIAL MEDIA NOMINATION FORM THE LEGISLATURE BRIT

S DO NOT FILL THE GAPS WORLD DEBATING CHAMPION COMES FROM HACKNEY DE

H FOR QUESTIONS WHO IS BEHIND THIS? INDIAN ELECTIONS OF 2014 TO S

HE SYSTEM BROKEN? PROVOCATION EXAGGERATION MONITORING FERGUSON DO TI

INDS WORKING FROM WITHIN ALTERNATIVE FACTS ARE THEY TRUSWORT

ULISM ON THE RISE IN THE WEST AT THE MOMENT? ARE THEY CREDIBLE? GET

ORY CONQUER SOCIAL MEDIA SPEAK LOUD AND PROUD AVOID THE HYPNOTIST

G PEOPLE OFF THE UNIONS? PROVIDE TEMPLATES FOR THE LETTER MAKE

ELECTION AGENT SHARE YOUR CAMPAIGN ON SOCIAL MEDIA NOMINATION F

OUR ARM RELAX YOUR HANDS DO NOT FILL THE GAPS WORLD DEBATING CHAMPI

S WHO IS BEHIND THIS? INDIAN ELECTIONS OF 2014 TO SLANT THE FA

EN? PROVOCATION EXAGGERATION MONITORING FERGUSON DO THEY HAVE A RI

FROM WITHIN ALTERNATIVE FACTS ARE THEY TRUSWORTHY? EDITING A

SE IN THE WEST AT THE MOMENT? ARE THEY CREDIBLE? GET YOUR MESSAG

OCIAL MEDIA SPEAK LOUD AND PROUD AVOID THE HYPNOTISTS CRACK DEBAT

THE UNIONS? PROVIDE TEMPLATES FOR THE LETTER MAKE YOUR GOAL CLE

ENT SHARE YOUR CAMPAIGN ON SOCIAL MEDIA NOMINATION FORM THE LEGISL

YOUR HANDS DO NOT FILL THE GAPS WORLD DEBATING CHAMPION COMES FROM

ST CASH FOR QUESTIONS WHO IS BEHIND THIS? INDIAN ELECTIONS OF 20-

ER IS THE SYSTEM BROKEN? PROVOCATION EXAGGERATION MONITORING FERGUSO

GING MINDS WORKING FROM WITHIN ALTERNATIVE FACTS ARE THEY TRUS

CONCLUSION

So, have you found your voice? I'm hoping that by now you're clanging the stop button on the bus of daily life, eager to jump off and make some noise.

So what's on your agenda?

→ Does politics need to be taught more widely?

→ Will you lobby your MP about lowering the voting age?

→ Could a sit-in help prevent the closure of a local community centre?

→ Can you join a march on climate change?

It doesn't matter what you're passionate about – it's time to get out there. And now that you're ready to take action, we can think about some last-minute strategies.

Get off your ass

Work out what you care about and get going – whether it's putting an idea out on social media and seeing what reaction you get or grabbing a bunch of mates and making some noise. It doesn't matter how you start – just start!

Get inspired

Read about the activists who sat where you are right now but went on to become campaigning heroes. You're not alone – there are hundreds of stories of Davids who went up against Goliaths and won. It's always good to keep these tales in your back pocket for the days when you feel you're not making any progress. Stories of solidarity will keep pushing you on!

It's all about timing

There is a shift from the traditional powers of corporations, governments and mainstream media to the new power of social media. Now is the perfect time to take advantage of this opportunity – you understand social networks way better than the older generations.

Embrace social media and harness it in more effective ways than your opponents.

Recruit some allies

Allies could be similar groups campaigning for the same change. They could be like-minded people with a different agenda that works well alongside your own, such as clean beaches and anti-pollution campaigns. Or they might be politicians who just want to look good. Either way, network, find them and work with them.

Watch out for pitfalls

Beware of the fakes and the traps. You don't want to tarnish all your hard work with false facts or unreliable research. Triple-check your sources.

Ride the curve

There might be key times to protest or petition that fit in with events or changes. The news agenda relies on 'pegs' for journalists to hang stories on, such as key developments in a story, an announcement or an anniversary. If you want publicity for your action, look out for these pegs and make a plan around them. You'll get more coverage in the mainstream media.

Start small, think big

Your issue might seem local but have bigger potential – consider whether your campaign could benefit a wider community than the one you first thought of.

Start local but think global. One voice can be heard around the world on YouTube!

Stay the course

Campaigns are rarely quick and easy. They take stamina, patience, resilience and self-belief. If you feel strongly about something, don't be knocked off-course. Set your goals and stick to them. Keep on keeping on!

P.S. REMEMBER:

There are bullies in every society who force their will on a few individuals, whole communities or entire nations. And there are young people who risk persecution or worse if they speak out against these bullies. But still they speak.

Is something wrong in your world?
You have a voice.
Use it.

ON THE RISE IN THE WEST AT THE MOMENT? ARE THEY CREDIBLE?
NQUER SOCIAL MEDIA SPEAK LOUD AND PROUD AVOID THE HYPNOTI
PLE OFF THE UNIONS? PROVIDE TEMPLATES FOR THE LETTER MAR
TION AGENT SHARE YOUR CAMPAIGN ON SOCIAL MEDIA NOMINATION
RM RELAX YOUR HANDS DO NOT FILL THE GAPS WORLD DEBATING CHA

VIST CASH FOR QUESTIONS WHO IS BEHIND THIS? INDIAN ELECTIO
WER IS THE SYSTEM BROKEN? PROVOCATION EXAGGERATION MONITORING
NGING MINDS WORKING FROM WITHIN ALTERNATIVE FACTS ARE TH
HY IS POPULISM ON THE RISE IN THE WEST AT THE MOMENT? ARE THE
YOUR STORY CONQUER SOCIAL MEDIA SPEAK LOUD AND PROUD AVOID
NG YOUNG PEOPLE OFF THE UNIONS? PROVIDE TEMPLATES FOR TH
R VOICE? ELECTION AGENT SHARE YOUR CAMPAIGN ON SOCIAL MEDI
CROSS YOUR ARM RELAX YOUR HANDS DO NOT FILL THE GAPS WORLD
WHO IS BEHIND THIS? INDIAN ELECTIONS OF 2014 TO SLANT TH
? PROVOCATION EXAGGERATION MONITORING FERGUSON DO THEY HAVE
ROM WITHIN ALTERNATIVE FACTS ARE THEY TRUSTWORTHY? EDIT
IN THE WEST AT THE MOMENT? ARE THEY CREDIBLE? GET YOUR ME
IAL MEDIA SPEAK LOUD AND PROUD AVOID THE HYPNOTISTS CRACK
E UNIONS? PROVIDE TEMPLATES FOR THE LETTER MAKE YOUR GOA
T SHARE YOUR CAMPAIGN ON SOCIAL MEDIA NOMINATION FORM THE L
OUR HANDS DO NOT FILL THE GAPS WORLD DEBATING CHAMPION COMES

VIST CASH FOR QUESTIONS WHO IS BEHIND THIS? INDIAN ELECTIC
OWER IS THE SYSTEM BROKEN? PROVOCATION EXAGGERATION MONITORIN
NGING MINDS WORKING FROM WITHIN ALTERNATIVE FACTS ARE T
HY IS POPULISM ON THE RISE IN THE WEST AT THE MOMENT? ARE THE
YOUR STORY CONQUER SOCIAL MEDIA SPEAK LOUD AND PROUD AVOID
ING YOUNG PEOPLE OFF THE UNIONS? PROVIDE TEMPLATES FOR TH
R VOICE? ELECTION AGENT SHARE YOUR CAMPAIGN ON SOCIAL MED
CROSS YOUR ARM RELAX YOUR HANDS DO NOT FILL THE GAPS WORLD

QUESTIONS WHO IS BEHIND THIS? INDIAN ELECTIONS OF 2014 TO
TEM BROKEN? PROVOCATION EXAGGERATION MONITORING FERGUSON DO
WORKING FROM WITHIN ALTERNATIVE FACTS ARE THEY TRUSTWOR
ON THE RISE IN THE WEST AT THE MOMENT? ARE THEY CREDIBLE? C
NQUER SOCIAL MEDIA SPEAK LOUD AND PROUD AVOID THE HYPNOTIS
PLE OFF THE UNIONS? PROVIDE TEMPLATES FOR THE LETTER MAK
TION AGENT SHARE YOUR CAMPAIGN ON SOCIAL MEDIA NOMINATION
RM RELAX YOUR HANDS DO NOT FILL THE GAPS WORLD DEBATING CHAM
LD ACTIVIST CASH FOR QUESTIONS WHO IS BEHIND THIS? INDIAN E
N SUPEPOWER IS THE SYSTEM BROKEN? PROVOCATION EXAGGERATION MON
HT CHANGING MINDS WORKING FROM WITHIN ALTERNATIVE FACTS

RESOURCES

Get political

assembly.wales
Official website of the National Assembly for Wales

greenparty.org.uk
Website of the Green Party of England and Wales – it has links to its Scotland and Northern Ireland sister parties

mydup.com
Home of the Democratic Unionist Party

niassembly.gov.uk
Official website of the Northern Ireland Assembly

parliament.scot
Official website of the Scottish Parliament

parliament.uk
Official website of the UK Parliament, including info on the House of Commons and the House of Lords

plaid.cymru
Home of Plaid Cymru

publicwhip.org.uk
Not-for-profit website that lets you see how MPs, Lords and MSPs voted on any given issue

sdlp.ie
Website of the Social Democratic and Labour Party

sinnfein.ie
Home of Sinn Féin

snp.org
Website of the Scottish National Party

theyworkforyou.com
Politically neutral site that aims to make it easy to follow politics. Contains information on every politician in the UK and Scottish parliaments, and the Wales and Northern Ireland assemblies.

ukip.org
Home of the UK Independence Party

uup.org
Website of the Ulster Unionist Party

Become an activist

38degrees.org.uk
One of the UK's biggest campaigning communities

amnesty.org.uk
UK website for Amnesty International, a global human rights campaigning organisation

avaaz.org
A global online activist network

bitetheballot.co.uk
A not-for-profit empowering young people to become change-makers

do-it.org
Do-it Trust is the UK's national volunteering database

gvi.co.uk
The Global Volunteering Initiative sends volunteers to community development and conservation projects around the world

http://www.parliament.uk/get-involved/elections/standing
Discover how to stand as a candidate in a general election

https://petition.parliament.uk
The official UK Government and Parliament petitions site

ukyouthparliament.org.uk
Site of the UK Youth Parliament, where 11–18-year-olds can be elected to campaign for social change

volunteeringmatters.org.uk
A UK-specific organisation that helps volunteers support local communities in need

votesat16.org
Site campaigning for the UK voting age to be lowered to 16

worksmart.org.uk/tools/union-finder
Useful tool provided by the Trades Union Congress, to help workers find unions in their company or field

Stay informed

fullfact.org
The UK's independent factchecking charity

newsnow.co.uk
A leading independent news aggregator in the UK

theweek.co.uk
Website that aims to distil breaking news into easily understood, bitesize chunks free of opinion or bias

WORKING FROM WITHIN ALTERNATIVE FACTS ARE THEY TRUST WO
ON THE RISE IN THE WEST AT THE MOMENT? ARE THEY CREDIBLE?
ONQUER SOCIAL MEDIA SPEAK LOUD AND PROUD AVOID THE HYPNOTIS
PLE OFF THE UNIONS? PROVIDE TEMPLATES FOR THE LETTER MAK
TION AGENT SHARE YOUR CAMPAIGN ON SOCIAL MEDIA NOMINATION
RM RELAX YOUR HANDS DO NOT FILL THE GAPS WORLD DEBATING CHAM

VIST CASH FOR QUESTIONS WHO IS BEHIND THIS? INDIAN ELECTIO
WER IS THE SYSTEM BROKEN? PROVOCATION EXAGGERATION MONITORING
NGING MINDS WORKING FROM WITHIN ALTERNATIVE FACTS ARE TH
HY IS POPULISM ON THE RISE IN THE WEST AT THE MOMENT? ARE THEY
YOUR STORY CONQUER SOCIAL MEDIA SPEAK LOUD AND PROUD AVOID
NG YOUNG PEOPLE OFF THE UNIONS? PROVIDE TEMPLATES FOR THE
VOICE? ELECTION AGENT SHARE YOUR CAMPAIGN ON SOCIAL MEDI
CROSS YOUR ARM RELAX YOUR HANDS DO NOT FILL THE GAPS WORLD
WHO IS BEHIND THIS? INDIAN ELECTIONS OF 2014 TO SLANT TH
? PROVOCATION EXAGGERATION MONITORING FERGUSON DO THEY HAVE
ROM WITHIN ALTERNATIVE FACTS ARE THEY TRUSTWORTHY? EDIT
IN THE WEST AT THE MOMENT? ARE THEY CREDIBLE? GET YOUR ME
IAL MEDIA SPEAK LOUD AND PROUD AVOID THE HYPNOTISTS CRACK
E UNIONS? PROVIDE TEMPLATES FOR THE LETTER MAKE YOUR GOAL
T SHARE YOUR CAMPAIGN ON SOCIAL MEDIA NOMINATION FORM THE L
OUR HANDS DO NOT FILL THE GAPS WORLD DEBATING CHAMPION COMES

VIST CASH FOR QUESTIONS WHO IS BEHIND THIS? INDIAN ELECTIO
OWER IS THE SYSTEM BROKEN? PROVOCATION EXAGGERATION MONITORIN
NGING MINDS WORKING FROM WITHIN ALTERNATIVE FACTS ARE T
HY IS POPULISM ON THE RISE IN THE WEST AT THE MOMENT? ARE THE
YOUR STORY CONQUER SOCIAL MEDIA SPEAK LOUD AND PROUD AVOID
ING YOUNG PEOPLE OFF THE UNIONS? PROVIDE TEMPLATES FOR TH
R VOICE? ELECTION AGENT SHARE YOUR CAMPAIGN ON SOCIAL MED
CROSS YOUR ARM RELAX YOUR HANDS DO NOT FILL THE GAPS WORLD

QUESTIONS WHO IS BEHIND THIS? INDIAN ELECTIONS OF 2014 TO
TEM BROKEN? PROVOCATION EXAGGERATION MONITORING FERGUSON DO
WORKING FROM WITHIN ALTERNATIVE FACTS ARE THEY TRUSTWOR
ON THE RISE IN THE WEST AT THE MOMENT? ARE THEY CREDIBLE?
NQUER SOCIAL MEDIA SPEAK LOUD AND PROUD AVOID THE HYPNOTIS
PLE OFF THE UNIONS? PROVIDE TEMPLATES FOR THE LETTER MAK
TION AGENT SHARE YOUR CAMPAIGN ON SOCIAL MEDIA NOMINATION
RM RELAX YOUR HANDS DO NOT FILL THE GAPS WORLD DEBATING CHAM
OLD ACTIVIST CASH FOR QUESTIONS WHO IS BEHIND THIS? INDIAN E
N SUPEPOWER IS THE SYSTEM BROKEN? PROVOCATION EXAGGERATION MON
HT CHANGING MINDS WORKING FROM WITHIN ALTERNATIVE FACTS

INDEX

A

B

C

M

Major, John 58
march 109, 133, 134, 135, 147, 149, 162, 164, 229, 279
　Women's March 136, 137
May, Theresa 11, 29, 65, 66, 126
McConnell, Jack 107
Member of Parliament *see* MP
Member of Scottish Parliament *see* MSP
Metropolitan police *see* police
Miliband, Ed 65, 111, 112
miner's strike *see* strike
Modi, Narendra President 219
Morar, Natalia 216
MP 21, 26, 29, 32, 33, 34, 35, 38, 39, 40, 47, 50, 52, 55, 56,
　57, 58, 59, 60, 61, 78, 90, 91, 94, 95, 100, 104, 105, 113,
　115, 157, 203, 264, 268, 270, 279
MSP 39 , 107
Mugabe, Robert 160

N

Naief, Abazid 79
National Health Service *see* NHS
NHS 22, 23, 31, 99, 270
Northern Ireland 25, 29, 44, 269
Northern Ireland Assembly 25, 44

O

O'Sullivan, Ronnie 112
Obama, Barack 111, 240
occupation 141, 147, 149, 187
opinion poll *see* poll
opposition 32, 158, 160, 246, 250, 270

P

Parliament, Houses of 21, 26, 28, 32, 38, 39, 44, 55, 57, 58,
　61, 68, 88, 89, 90, 91, 95, 105, 107, 117, 122, 126, 138, 216,
　223, 272
　hung Parliament 28, 67
　Scottish Parliament 44, 107

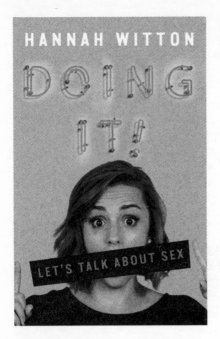

Paperback
April 2017
978 1 5263 6003 8

Doing It
by Hannah Witton

Sexting. Virginity. Consent. The Big O ... Let's face it, doing it can be tricksy. I don't know anyone (including myself) who has sex all figured out. So I've written a book full of honest, hilarious (and awkward) anecdotes, confessions and revelations. And because none of us have all the answers, I've invited some friends and fellow YouTubers to talk about their sexuality, too.

Paperback
November 2017
978 1 5263 6068 7

Trans Mission
by Alex Bertie

I like pugs, doughnuts and tattoos. I sleep with my socks on. Oh, and I'm transgender. That's the bit that usually throws people. Being trans is only one part of who I am, but it's played a huge role in shaping me. Over the last six years, I've come out to my family, changed my name, battled the NHS, started taking male hormones and have had top surgery. My quest to a beard is almost complete. This is my story.

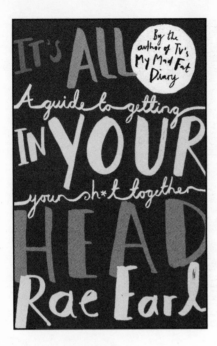

On the book cover:
IT'S ALL
By the author of Tv's My Mad Fat Diary
A guide to getting
IN YOUR
your sh*t together
HEAD
Rae Earl

Paperback
August 2017
978 1 5263 0002 7

It's All In Your Head
by Rae Earl

As a teenager, I was very adept at hiding my OCD, my anxiety, my depression and my eating disorders behind a smile and a big sack of silly. And that is why I've written this book. Because I hate to think of any teen going through what I did, and feeling like they need to hide it. This is a book to break down taboos, to start conversations, to help you talk about things that seem impossible. You are not alone.

Hardback
January 2018
978 1 5263 0023 2

Rebel Voices
by Eve Lloyd Knight
and Louise Kay Stewart

A stunning celebration of the campaigners who fought for women's right to vote. Discover the 40,000 Russian women who marched, and the Kuwaiti women who protested via text message. Women climbed mountains, walked a lion through of Paris, and starved themselves, all in the name of having a voice. Meet the women worldwide who rioted, rallied and refused to give up.